Misfit

MINU PARTI

BALBOA.PRESS
A DIVISION OF HAY HOUSE

Balboa Press books may be ordered through booksellers or by contacting:

Balboa Press
A Division of Hay House
1663 Liberty Drive
Bloomington, IN 47403
www.balboapress.com
1 (877) 407-4847

Print information available on the last page.

ISBN: 978-1-9822-3843-8 (sc)
ISBN: 978-1-9822-3842-1 (e)

Balboa Press rev. date: 11/19/2019

This book is dedicated to Minu's
daughters and her husband

Introduction

This story begins in a land of culture, India. It is the story of a little girl who grew into a beautiful, accomplished woman with two daughters of her own. In the beginning, the little girl's life was simple and sheltered, with loving parents who always tried to fulfill her little demands. Living in an affluent section of a great city, surrounded by people of all races and classes, she grew to have many interests and triumphs as she developed a range of talents both artistic and intellectual.

As a child and teen, her artistic side predominated, and she dreamed of someday becoming famous. And who can say she could not have been, for she was a supremely photogenic model who, as a young woman, became a successful print model in New York City and internationally. She was even given an explicit invitation to become a movie actress. But the Great River of Life took her on a course where she was able only to flirt with a fame that remained an island out of reach. As a result, her intellectual side eventually came into prominence.

At a young age, she got married to a husband her parents chose for her, and she is grateful to her parents' for their decision because he is a great guy. She became an excellent wife, learning all about her husband's likes and dislikes, molding herself to his life, and giving up her own personality. She learned to live his life and is still living his life. Professionally, she also followed her husband, who became an outstanding cardiologist. Inspired by him to enter the Health field, she earned a university Master's degree in Health Science and became a skilled physician assistant.

But there was a third side to this young woman, one that came to the fore when she gave birth to two girls. This side was that of an intense and abiding Motherly Love that nourished, nurtured, and created the opportunities that enabled her children to become accomplished young women.

This is the story of Minu, the story of her dreams, accomplishments, sacrifices, and enduring spirit.

A Childhood Full of Love

As a little girl, Minu grew like a flower in the sheltered garden of her family. Always full of laughter and life, she was constantly commenting on whatever might be happening, or laughing merrily at something her father said that tickled her funny bone. Sometimes, though, she was curious, her face turning oh so serious, as she asked her mother question after question about how things were done, and why they were done in a certain way. Why this, why that, why, why, why, until her mother said, in exasperation, "Because that is just the way we do things, Minu!"

Minu was delicate, her skin like porcelain, and her parents loved her beyond words. She lit up her parents' life. More than once they told her that when she was born she was the most beautiful, the most exquisite baby girl they had ever seen.

Her father and mother worked very hard to provide the

best for their family, and she lived comfortably in the city with her brother and younger sister. She was surrounded by household help, including a cook and a nanny, and never had to do any work around the home, which was the normal way of living for the upper middle class in India. Her life was simple and protected. Her home was a sanctuary where the days were all about school, playtime, and homework. Her daily routine consisted of traveling by school bus to school and back home. After coming home, she had a few hours of free time to play, then homework, and then the day was over.

Her parents were very involved in their children's upbringing. In that era, there was tremendous respect for parents. Children never questioned them, as they were sure the parents always had the children's best interests in mind. And indeed, Minu's parents did. Her mom and dad were judicious and intelligent in their children's upbringing, understanding that each child had his or her own individual personality and taking that into account in dealing with the child. And her parents enforced strict rules:

> No TV on school nights
> Very limited TV on weekends
> Be indoors before dark
> No drinking before 21

There was also no going out to movies, except rarely. She recalls vividly her dad and mom taking her, her brother, and her sister to dinner at a nice restaurant and then a movie as it was her parents' anniversary. This was a big treat for all of them.

Yet Minu's parents were crazy about their children, often telling them how proud they were of them and showing their love in countless ways, making it obvious that their kids were their world. They constantly worked to build strong character and values in their children, encouraging them to be busy with various activities, teaching them that their actions had consequences good or bad. They encouraged Minu and her siblings to do their best and act responsibly at every step, to get good grades, be independent thinkers, believe in themselves, and pursue happy, productive, successful lives when they became adults. They never compared their children to other kids, never gossiped or made negative remarks about other people.

As the middle child, Minu had to learn to balance the dual role of being younger sister to one sibling and older sister to the other. For some reason, she couldn't seem to get the balance quite right. Though she loved her brother and sister, she felt they were closer to each other than to her. As a result, she was always trying to please one or the other or both of them. One strategy she used to get on their good side was to bribe them in an attempt to gain their favor. The bribe came from the weekly allowance she received, along with her siblings, a small allowance that varied depending on each child's behavior. When her brother and sister spent their allowances and found themselves without money, she saw opportunity knocking. That's when she stepped in with her saved allowance and bought a round of yummy chocolates for everyone. She loved to be The Chocolate Provider— surely rising high in her brother and sister's estimation!

Meals were sometimes a challenge, as from an early age

Minu was a picky eater. Her parents, for the most part, put up with her likes and dislikes in food, telling their cook to prepare what Minu liked. The norm of the house—a family ritual—was for the family to eat dinner together, her father at the head of the table, as everyone talked about their day. The three children were taught to never waste food. They had to clean their plates first before they could have any seconds. To impress their father, the siblings had an unwritten competition among themselves to be the one to first reach a spotlessly clean plate. For a while, Minu had an advantage by the fact that her dog sat on the floor next to her at the dining table. If the crafty little girl did not particularly like what was on her plate, she would sneak bits of food to the dog when no one seemed to be paying attention. All went well until one evening when the dog turned its nose up to what she tried to feed it. When her mother found the uneaten morsel on the floor, questioning ensued and the truth came out. The dog was banished from around the dining table during meals, and Minu had to compete with her brother and sister in the plate-cleaning contest without the assistance of her former ally.

Her father was a strict disciplinarian, a man of principle and manners who emphasized to his children the importance of integrity and poise, doing well in school, always honoring their elders, and finding goodness in every soul. His opinions were well considered and his word was final. But he was fair in his decisions, always taking into account the well-being of the family as a whole and each member of the family.

Her father was also a loving man, and Minu was the apple of his eye, his princess, and he always made that clear to her. He liked for her to read to him during the evening after dinner while he relaxed in his easy chair. The book he chose for her to read sometimes had a few difficult words that she had to puzzle through, and he would say "Good, good!" when she finally conquered a word. Sometimes he closed his eyes as she read. One evening, after a few minutes of his silence, glancing up occasionally to see his eyes shut and his breathing steady, she became convinced that he had fallen asleep. So, she felt safe when, coming to a difficult word, she simply skipped it. Right then, her father's eyes flashed open as he said, in his deep voice, "Read again!" At that instant, a jolt of electricity ran through her. There was nothing for her to do but to struggle with the difficult word, feeling confused and wondering whether her father had been pretending to sleep or had simply woken up at just the right time.

Her mother had a softer, artistic side, and was a nurturer. Her mother loved music and played the sitar and tabla, two traditional Indian instruments. The sweet and evocative sounds of her mother playing the sitar sometimes wafted through their home and led little Minu to dream of lovely mountain scenes with blue skies and clear crystal water cascading down the hillsides. Her mother's gentle playing worked its magic by bringing little Minu to love music.

Minu was raised in a Western way. Her mother wanted to expose her children to the world and not raise them in a bubble or a box, and so she liked to take them on outings. Occasionally, she would take the three children to India Gate, an amusement complex, for boating and various fun activities. Minu loved it there. Visiting the world outside always made her feel joyful, as it seemed filled with exciting places to be explored, unlimited treasures to be uncovered.

Her parents were active socially and sometimes on the weekend would go out in the evening to visit friends while the kids stayed home with Nanny. Just as often, the friends were the ones visiting. Minu loved those evenings, the excitement of preparation, with everyone in such a bustle beforehand. She was eager to be of help in getting ready for the guests and loved to be assigned the duty of preparing the table and making sure the correct silverware was out and properly arranged. Other times, her parents stayed home with their children on the weekends, and Minu loved those times most, the family all at home and relaxing together throughout the day and evening. So close.

But not all was rosy, as Minu was a delicate child and her health not always the best. In her late preteens, a strange and dreadful cycle ensued when she was attacked by painful and long-lasting migraine headaches every month at about the same time. Suddenly waking out of a peaceful sleep in the middle of the night, she felt the excruciating pain burning into her head. A few minutes later it drove her out of her bed and into the bathroom to vomit. Afterwards, pain undiminished, she called out plaintively to her mother and father for help. They always came right away, but could do nothing except provide a few mostly ineffective standard pain relievers, then sit by her bed and comfort her as the headache ravaged on. Typically, the migraine lasted for 12 hours, half a day lost in pain. Deeply worried about the severity and frequency of the headaches, her parents took her to the best neurologist they could find, but he could offer no cure. So, the family learned to live with the reality of the migraines, every one of them—but most of all Minu—dreading the eruption of the next one. Sometimes, as she lay in bed feeling as if her head were in the unrelenting grip of a horrible vise, she wondered if the migraines would continue all her life so that she would never be free for long from the monthly harrowing pain. The thought always tortured her, making the headaches all the worse. Then one month, just after she turned 13, the migraine failed to appear as expected, and then again the next month. And with as little explanation as when they had appeared, the headaches were gone. A physician later suggested to her parents that they had somehow been hormonally triggered.

Minu's parents taught their children always to aim high, insisting that there was nothing they couldn't achieve if they put their minds to it. The little girl took those lessons to heart and lay sometimes in bed imagining what she might be. She had not failed to realize, at a very young age, that there were two sets of rules for boys and girls. Boys had more liberty than girls. As she grew, she learned that girls had to be home before it got dark and could have no late evening activities. Boys could stay out later. As she lay in bed dreaming of the future, she sometimes wondered if it were really true that she could achieve anything, because it seemed that some roles were only for males. But then she decided it did not matter to her, because whatever she decided to become would probably be something artistic, something very compatible with being a girl, a woman. It didn't take long for her imaginings to bring her to the conclusion that her proper role in life was to be famous.

She practiced for what she felt would be her destiny—being famous— by singing and dancing about the house. She also incorporated her dreams into her playtime. Her sister gladly obliged by acting out the role of a reporter interviewing her. With notebook in hand, her sister asked her what her life was like as a superstar. "Wonderful!" she replied. "I love to sing and dance and I appreciate all my fans so much," all the while imagining crowds of admirers tripping over one another to ask for her autograph. Sometimes she was a famous singer, sometimes a dancer, sometimes both. Always in a fantasy land. Or, maybe better, always trying her best to make the beautiful colors and emotions of fantasy part of her existence.

The older Minu got, the more she loved life. As she grew into her early teens, her dreams were nourished by her mother wanting her to learn classical dancing and to play an instrument. Always full of energy and with a passion to learn new things, she followed her mother's wishes and took up classical dancing and the guitar. The sometimes soft, sometimes fiery character of the guitar seemed to match her personality very well, and she found herself dreaming, during one short period, of becoming a gypsy, her only aim just to sing and dance and play her guitar for others.

It was difficult for her to sit still for long, even for the guitar. Every summer break she spent time with her cousins. Always a leader, never a follower, she would teach her cousins a dance number that they performed in front of their parents to enthusiastic applause. During summer breaks, she also joined various outside activities, one of which was riding. She loved riding horses, loved to feel the air against her face and the wind whipping through her hair as she rode as fast as she dared. The faster she rode, the more she felt like she was capturing some essential core of life. Ride over, she found it difficult to accept the fact that it was time to jump down from her horse. Why so soon?! She was sure she could ride that wonderful way all day long, all night, maybe forever.

Summers over and back in school, her interests and activities were wide ranging. She was good at sports and was on the high school girls' basketball team. But more and more, her interests trended toward the artistic. She took art courses, learned to paint, and found herself loving that. She continued her guitar lessons and added the banjo to her musical repertoire. And she became very involved in both theater and dancing at school. She started learning how good it was to experience being successful, as each year she felt she was making marked improvements in her dancing, becoming more graceful and agile and focused. Her teachers agreed, as she won awards on her dance performance several years in a row.

Receiving her first award, hearing her name spoken out loud as a winner, made her feel like she was being announced at some Gala Grand Opening. "Minu, Minu!" she heard a crowd call in her head. After receiving the award, she returned to her seat feeling proud and recognized—firmly on her way, she was sure, to Fame. Later, she also was given an award by the future Indian Prime Minister Vajpayee for having the highest scores in her classes.

Her dreams about becoming famous became stronger. She was still not sure what she would be famous for, but she was convinced she would become known in the world for something special, perhaps as a dancer, or actress, or singer. The problem was, she had no idea how to become famous, or what would be required to achieve her dream. She only knew that she craved to be known. All through her childhood she had loved life and exhibited high energy, and it seemed to her that living a life as a famous person in the performing arts, she could continue to live on that high energy level. It would be a most beautiful life, full of grace, wonderful artistic events, and accolades. But despite all she had learned about dance and the theatre, the awards, and her certainty that she had abundant talent, she just could not figure out the steps to follow to make her dreams come true.

Eventually, she finished high school and enrolled in college. She looked longingly at the offerings of Drama and Dance departments, but in the end decided to major in Economics, which was a far cry from dancing and music and acting. But her parents, especially her father, emphasized to her the importance of learning something practical that would enable her to find a good job. It wasn't difficult for her to accept her parents' views because she had always thirsted for knowledge and had an interest in many subjects, and she had always admired people with brains and substance who were not just fluff personalities. Economics was one of the fields that fascinated her. How did economies work? What helped businesses and people to prosper? These seemed like worthwhile questions to ask and answer. So, her dreams of being famous were laid aside, at least temporarily, and she worked hard at studying economics. And she did well. So well, in fact, that she passed her second year with the highest marks in her university.

She celebrated her achievement with her family, her mother and father very proud of her. But as she did so, laughing and talking—less a chatterbox now, and more a brilliant and talented young woman—young Minu had no idea that her life would soon change and take an entirely new direction.

Chapter 2

A Fateful Evening

M inu was in her second year at the university and doing well when one morning she received a signal that her life was about to change.

At breakfast her mom remarked, "Dear, you need to come home today right after your classes are finished. We have invited some guests to come visit with you. They will be arriving early. Please be home by 4:30. They should be here by 5:00."

Minu was surprised to hear that people were coming to see her in particular, and not her parents or the whole family.

"Guests coming to see *me*? Who is it?"

"A young man and his family," her mother replied. "A handsome young man. He's a doctor, an accomplished doctor from the United States. He grew up in Punjab, India, and has returned home to visit his parents. While he is here, he wants to meet several girls with the possibility of finding one he feels would make a compatible wife. His parents have told him about you, and he would like to meet you."

When her mom uttered the term "wife," the word hit Minu like a thunderbolt. Wife? She was not even 19 years old. She had over two years to go at the university before she got her degree. It was far too early for anyone to be considering her as a possible *wife*!

Minu quickly realized that what might be at stake in the meeting to be held that evening was that her parents were taking the first steps toward enrolling her in a traditional arranged marriage. Such marriages are common in India, with parents typically the ones to choose their son's or daughter's future spouse—usually with only a little input from the soon-to-be newlywed. True, if the son or daughter refuses the choice, the parents tend to respect that choice and will seek someone else. So, the marriage is not forced. However, the marriageable child can experience considerable pressure to accept the parents' choice of a mate.

Pressure comes not just from the parents but from society itself. In India, the accepted social viewpoint is that when it comes to the serious life choice of marriage, parents know best. The parents realize that their child, only recently an adult, has so far lived in a protected cocoon and understands little of the challenges life may bring. In making their choice, the parents are motivated solely by their desire for their son's or daughter's happiness. The girl's parents are interested in her suitor's accomplishments, his family values, and whether he will be able to provide a good life for their daughter. The young man's parents are interested in whether the girl will be a good helpmate for their son and a good mother.

Pressure may also come from other family members, who often play a significant role in bringing a couple together. In coordination with the parents, relatives may take the initiative to find, evaluate, and approve potential spouses for a young man or woman.

The young people usually meet for the first time under the supervision of their elders. The young man is typically looking for a girl who is beautiful and takes his breath away. The young woman is hoping for a man who is handsome and romantic. They talk for a while and get to know a few basics about each other. If they decide to abide by their parents' decision, they may marry while they are barely acquainted. The expectation is that they will develop a loving relationship over time.

All that day at school, Minu mulled the morning conversation over, her thoughts interlaced with what she knew about arranged marriages. None of her professors' lectures could find a place to settle in her mind as the strange word "wife" kept bouncing around in her head and spilling into her thoughts. How could she be someone's wife at this stage of her life? After much worry, she finally decided she would stay late and simply not be there for the evening meeting. She would find some excuse for having to stay at school until the visitors left. Problem solved!

That evening, she arrived home at 6:00, an hour after the scheduled visit. No one but her parents seemed to be there.

"You're late," her father accused her as soon as she entered. He was not smiling. Nor was her mother.

"I was assigned to do a report tomorrow and had to stay late to do research at the library," she explained, deploying the white lie she had concocted on the way home. As she said those words, she kept looking around to make sure no one else was there. She couldn't help but congratulate herself: *Thank goodness my strategy worked!*

"Hmmm," her father said with a grave tone. Her mother raised her eyebrows at her. Then all was silence.

Beginning to feel uncomfortable, she rushed to say, "I'm sorry I missed the visitors. I hope you're not angry."

Her father and mother looked at one another, and Minu thought she noticed a little smile passing between them.

Her father turned to her. "Not at all, angry," he said. He checked his watch. "In fact, you're just in time."

A moment later, there was a knock on the door.

"There they are," her mother said, as she realized that her shrewd parents had given her the wrong time for the meeting.

While her father went to answer the door, her mother rushed over to her. "Go freshen up and change your clothes. Put on that nice new sari we bought last weekend. Now hurry, hurry. Don't keep your visitors waiting."

She went to her room to do as she was told. There was no getting out of it now, no putting it off. She would have to meet this man and his family. In her room, she briefly considered the possibility of taking off all her makeup, putting on her ugliest and worst-fitting dress, and messing up her hair so the man would not like her. But she knew that if she came out like that, her mother would simply apologize to the guests and say that unfortunately it would take another few minutes before the one they came to see was ready. Then she would immediately march her daughter back to her room and oversee her getting ready for the visitors. Besides, it was a matter of pride. Minu always took great care in her appearance. It was her nature to always try to look her best. She wasn't about to change now.

She put on the sari her mother had selected, a beautiful turquoise color with shades of dark blue and black. After her mom tied the sari, Minu had no clue how to walk in it. She had never worn a sari before as she had always dressed in Western-style clothes. Somehow, she managed to walk without stumbling, but she put barely any makeup on and tied her hair back as she wanted to appear ugly to the man. In her heart, she thought she would be rejected by him as he was from the U.S. and must be looking for a very sharp, sexy woman for a wife. Before going out, she sent her sister to see the boy and check out his looks and style. When her sister came back, she said, "Didi, I don't see any boy, maybe he did not come." Minu replied, "No, Mom said he is there. Go look again." A minute or two later, her sister came back with the same answer. Later, Minu realized that her sister was 15 and was looking for a high school-looking boy, not a guy with glasses and moustache. Finally, she went out to meet the man whom her parents had decided might be a good match for her.

After introductions were complete and refreshments served, Minu sat quietly as the man's parents, as well as his sister-in-law and her father, extolled his virtues. He was 26, had recently finished medical school in the U.S. with high marks, and was now a doctor in New York City showing all the signs of having a successful medical career in his future. He had come back to India to find a life partner, had given himself two weeks to do so, and had already met a few girls and their families. He was, in fact, intent on not only finding a wife, but actually marrying her in those two weeks.

Minu hardly knew what to think as she listened to all this. The man seemed pleasant enough. Nice. Good looking. And she knew that her father, who always liked highly educated and hard-working guys, would be impressed with him. But she had never really entertained the thought of marriage. It seemed to her that it was much too early for that. She was doing well at the university. She enjoyed economics and often wondered what kind of job she would get once she earned her degree. And there was also her desire to somehow become famous. She needed time to work out how to make that happen. No way was she getting married now, with all her dreams still unfulfilled.

Once the man's family had finished their accolades, it was time for Minu's parents to sing the praises of their daughter. They pointed out that she too was brilliant, having earned excellent grades at the university as an economics major. She was accomplished in dance, played several musical instruments, had performed in plays, and was an all-around great "catch." And it went without saying that she was beautiful, well mannered, and cultured.

After a time, Minu and the young man retired to another room to talk for half an hour. The young man did almost all the talking. He told her briefly about his dream to be a successful physician in New York City and to have a nice home and supportive family. He said he knew exactly what he was looking for in a life partner. He wanted a girl who stayed at home and was non-professional. His wife was to be a housewife. He was against his wife working outside, as he was a traditional man and believed in providing for his family. His own mom never worked and was not educated. She managed household chores and raised children.

She pretended to listen to him, but his words were like a buzzing in her ears. For her part, she had little to say. What was there for her to say?

She had never thought of marriage before. She had no clear idea what she would want in a husband. She felt that in some ways she was still a child, not a grown woman of marriageable age. She wanted to stay where she felt she was—somewhere in between a child and a woman. There was so much about the world she still needed to learn. She was just too young!

But she nodded her head occasionally as the young man talked. She smiled and nodded, and it appeared to him that she was agreeing with him. After a half hour of talk, the couple returned to the other room. There were a few more interchanges, especially between her parents and the sister-in-law, who seemed to be running the show as the man's matchmaker, and her father, who was a good friend of Minu's dad and had been the one who originally recommended the boy to Minu's parents. As Minu sat there quietly and somewhat numb, she listened to the young man's side of the family pressure her parents for a decision, saying they had a train that evening to catch to go back to Amritsar, where it was assumed that there were few possibilities for the young man.

Minu's parents seemed confused. They had agreed to see the young man, since he was recommended by her dad's good friend, the father of the boy's sister-in-law; but they mentioned that she was still very young and they had never thought of her getting married before she finished her education. Still, her dad's friend pressed her parents, talking about how great the young man was and saying that sooner or later she had to get married, so why miss out on this great boy?'

Finally, the visitors left.

Thank goodness that's done, she thought. She ate a quick dinner while listening to her parents rave about the young man. They seemed happy that she was liked by the man's family. When asked what she thought of him, all she managed to say was that he seemed nice. Otherwise, she remained noncommittal. Soon after dinner, eager for the evening to be over, she announced she was ready for bed.

"I think he liked you," her mother said just before she retired. "Oh," was all she replied, as she thought, *I hope not.*

The next morning her hope was soon dismantled, as she received, through her parents, a marriage proposal from the young man.

Her mom was delighted, as she held to the Indian belief that marriages are made in heaven. She believed that everything that happens, happens for a reason, with it all decided and destined already. She was sure her daughter's marriage was destined to be and was blessed by heaven.

Her father, too, was pleased with the proposal. Neither of her parents saw any flaw in the boy and the family. The only slight misgiving was that their daughter did not speak the language Punjabi that the groom's side spoke. But they reasoned this objection away with the knowledge that their daughter would be going to live in the U.S., where English would be spoken. Language, they decided, would not be an issue. As for the matter of her having to adjust to a new country, she had been raised in a Western way, so her parents did not see that as a problem.

The marriage proposal was accepted.

The next few days were a whirlwind of preparation. Minu stopped going to her classes at the university. Instead of attending lectures and preparing assignments, her days were filled with shopping for wedding apparel, learning ceremonies, sending out invitations, going to hair salons, and making a hundred decisions about the wedding, most of them actually made by her father and mother.

One evening her soon-to-be husband took permission from her parents to take her to the movies. She went, as her parents insisted, but in middle of the movie she told him she wanted to go home to her parents. She was so innocent she had no idea how to act when going out on a date. All of this was so sudden that she was in shock. She did not want to get married, but she could not defy her parents' wishes.

Barely a week after the proposal, the wedding was held in the house where she grew up in Vasant Vihar. The wedding celebrations were in full force, though they were all a blur in Minu's eyes, everything seeming unreal. But the end result was that she was now a wife.

She and her husband spent just a few days together before he had to fly back to the U.S. They had agreed that she would stay in India to take her second-year final exams. In the meantime, her husband and she would complete the paperwork and requirements for her to join him stateside. He would call her regularly to talk to her, but she would giggle and had no clue what to say. Her dad saw her struggling and started coaching her, telling her what to say. He would say, "Tell him you love him." She would turn around and respond, "But I don't even know him!" To her, the idea of loving him was far-fetched. Yet, she would always end up saying she loved him.

Chapter 3

Challenges of a New World

I t took only a few months before the day arrived for her to fly to the U.S. to be with her husband, a man she so far barely knew. Her emotions were chaotic throughout those last few days before her flight, as she was both excited and petrified about what lay before her. She had always lived under her parents' wings and followed their rules, and she was excited that she would no longer have to answer to her parents, nor follow their rules and discipline. She was sad at the same time, as she was very attached to her parents and siblings and knew that she would miss them sorely. And she was full of anxiety about living in a new household, in a new country. She had barely a clue about her husband's likes and dislikes and worried about whether she would please him.

She wondered about her new country. Would people be friendly? How would she fit in to the society there? Many nights in bed leading up to her big trip, she lay imagining what her life would be like in America. She had heard much about New York and its social life. She fantasized about going to parties, one party after another, with bright and friendly people wearing expensive fashions. There would be music, dancing, cocktails, and brilliant conversation. As for where she would live, she pictured a life-size dollhouse with separate dining and living rooms, bedrooms, and balconies. She had seen photographs of the New York skyscrapers. Her building would be tall, almost to the clouds, and it would have a beautiful green rooftop garden with a little waterfall just outside that she could visit whenever she wanted. It would all be wonderful!

On the day of her flight, her life was packed into three bursting suitcases. After a very long flight on which her fantasies about her future life were projected onto the blue skies outside her window, she arrived in New York.

Her husband picked her up at the airport in a new green Monte Carlo car with white leather seats, which impressed her. But she was nervous as they drove toward their apartment. She had no clue about the apartment as he never sent any pictures. He was a man of few or no words, so all she knew was that he lived in Coney Island in Brooklyn. She was not used to his quiet manner as she and her siblings had always been very talkative.

When they arrived at the apartment, the first thing she noticed was that it wasn't in a skyscraper, but rather in a four- or five-story building, miles distant from the tall buildings populating Manhattan. And then she saw the apartment: smaller than her bedroom in India, with the kitchen right in the bedroom and a small, inadequate closet. She was informed it was called a "studio," a totally new concept for her.

She was confused. She had thought her husband was a successful doctor. This tiny apartment didn't look like success to her. Her husband explained that he was doing his residency and that the pay at this stage of his career was not much. His residency would be completed in the not-to-distant future, and he would be able to strike out on his own. Then he would be able to make a lot more money, and they could afford a much nicer apartment. Until then, this would be their home. Minu realized that her husband may have told her all this before, but she had not heard him. In any event, this was to be her home. Somehow, she had never thought about what marriage really was. She had imagined that her husband would treat her like royalty, worshipping the ground she walked on. Now she finally realized that she had to get out of her fantasy life and face reality. She did an about-face, quickly deciding that she would try hard to make the best of her new situation.

It wasn't easy. One issue that kept troubling her in the early days of her marriage was cooking. She had no servants now, no cook, and she had never learned any household skills back in India. All she knew was how to instruct the servants and tell them what she liked to eat. She didn't want to have to learn household work or to cook. In her mind, it was servants who did that. Now it was her job.

But she had no idea what to feed her husband. The grocery store seemed overwhelming to her at first. Cooking remained a challenge. Her husband was doing hid internal medicine residency at Coney Island Hospital and was gone for long hours, and she would wait patiently without a clue about what to cook for herself and him. She started eating junk food as it tasted good and she did not have to cook it for herself. When her husband was home, they often ate fast food as money was tight and they felt they had little choice.

Slowly, she started to learn cooking, often asking her mom for help. She had no idea of the names of spices or beans. She described beans by their color as "black dahl," "orange dahl," and so on. She felt she had been given an enormous change in her life and a huge new role that she had to adjust to in a very short period of time.

As for the social life she had imagined would be so wonderful in New York, she quickly learned how mistaken she had been. Her husband had ties to the Indian community in New York, and soon after arriving, Minu started meeting his friends. These meetings and gatherings often felt strained to her, as the majority of her husband's friends came from small towns back home and backgrounds very different from her own. She quickly began to realize that being from the same country does not mean everyone's upbringing or thought processes are the same. She had never been self-conscious about her own upbringing and status, but her new so-called friends seemed to take pleasure in bringing it to her attention. Many of their comments had a subtext of criticism, often not at all subtle: "Oh, you are from Delhi. You people from the city always seem to act as if you are better." Yet in her naïveté, she at first did not understand what they were trying to say. Were they complimenting or insulting her?

From day one she was not welcomed by his friends. They were from the same town, Punjab, and there was a language barrier and a cultural difference. Not all Indians are alike: every state in India has its own dialect, and it didn't help that she did not speak or understand Punjabi, which most of the other wives spoke. While she tried her best to fit in, this language barrier made it more difficult. She also had to accommodate herself to the practice of the women not sitting or mingling with the men at social gatherings. That wasn't at all like what happened at social gatherings her parents had attended. There, women and men sat and laughed and ate together. Certainly, there were times when the women and men at those past gatherings would separate into groups for their respective gossip periods— but not for the entire evening! She decided the gatherings she was attending in New York were like a replay of high school. The ladies from Punjab made fun of her as she did not speak or comprehend Punjabi. They also judged her on her dressing-up style, which was very Western. Failing to realize that every household's dynamics are different, they laughed at her when she told them she did not drink tea or coffee in morning, as her parents never allowed it. Instead, at her parents' house they ate a good breakfast, which was usually corn flakes cereal or eggs and toast in the morning with Bournvita- flavored milk. Yet, due to the Punjab ladies' judgments, once Minu started drinking tea in mornings she felt very grown up and happy.

From day one she was not welcomed by his friends. Their was a language barrier. And his friends were from same town at home Punjab. Their was culture difference also. Not all Indian are alike. Every state in India has their own dialect

The bottom line is that she was mocked by the Punjab ladies at every step. At home, after attending a social event, her husband would ask if she had a good time. "No," was her usual answer. "No, I didn't. How could I? Sitting there with a group of women mostly talking in a language I don't understand, with none of them making the slightest effort to involve me in their conversations. And when I did try to make some conversation in English, I felt like I was barely tolerated. What was there to enjoy?"

It also did not help that even though hers was an arranged marriage, she was not well accepted by her in-laws. She could not understand why. How could they just decide not to like her? She was hardly a 19-year-old kid. She took some heart in the thought that eventually, they would surely accept her more fully as the bottom line was that she was their son's choice. At least she hoped they would.

Alone in their apartment, Minu spent many hours recalling her life in India. She missed her home and family terribly. The rules her parents had laid down for her did not seem so bad. She longed to go back and live by those rules again.

Her husband could not help but see her homesickness. Her longing to go back to India was so great that he agreed that she could go back for three months. He would miss her, but in his residency he was hardly ever home. Besides, she told him, once she was back in India, she would be able to learn to cook better from the family's cook.

She flew back and joyously flew into the arms of her mother and father at the airport. True to her word, she immediately started learning everything the cook could teach her. Her mother even signed her up for lessons from a cooking school so she could impress her husband when she returned to the U.S.

The time was wonderful, but it flew by far too fast. After three months, it was time again to leave. This time, it was harder than ever to leave her mom and dad and siblings. Another long melancholy flight. Back in the states, homesick again, she made it a point to write her family a letter every single night, describing how she spent her day.

Back in her new home in America, still homesick for her family in India, Minu was not very happy. At least not at first. As in many arranged marriages, the couple had become man and wife while barely knowing each other. Arranged marriages do not start with a honeymoon period—that comes later as the two people adjust to each other and gradually fall in love. There are often many conflicts during the first year or two, which was the case for Minu and her husband. Both partners were used to their own family's ways and had their own convictions, and both were frustrated with the newness of life as a couple. During the adjustment period, they faced the challenge of learning to understand, accept, and appreciate each other's differences in personalities and what each partner needed for happiness.

In the beginning, plenty of arguments arose as they tried to fit together. Minu began to realize that she and her husband were opposite in their thought processes. Her husband from day one was quiet, determined, calm, and cool. She, too, was determined, but in no way cool or calm. She was all over the map, with a temper lit by a short fuse. As a result, they would disagree and quarrel over issues big and little. Fortunately, both were resilient and committed to their marriage, and soon smoke from the latest blow-up would settle down.

The theme of many arguments was Minu's need to get out of the tiny studio apartment where she spent so much time alone. When her husband had a little time off during the evening, she yearned to go out and do something different, have fun together, maybe go to a nice place with music where they could dance. But he usually showed little interest, in part because he worked such long and odd hours at his internship.

"We hardly ever go out!" she would complain. "My mother and father were always going out with friends or inviting people over. We had wonderful dinner parties, everyone laughing and happy. And here I am stuck every night in this tiny apartment! I'm so tired of it."

"You are from a different world," her husband replied. "We don't have the money to go out wining and dining and dancing all the time."

"I don't know what you mean by a different world," she answered. "It's the only world I knew. And I miss it!"

"I know you do," he replied. "Someday we'll have more money, a better life. Just be patient."

Eventually, the argument would fade away into the evening and the growing affection between the two people would take over. But a day or two later, while alone in their apartment, Minu would find herself again reflecting on her situation: *I guess in Indian culture when you are married, your dreams are not yours anymore. Your husband's dreams are yours. His life is yours. The wife's individuality—my individuality—is gone.* That evening, as likely as not, another quarrel would erupt.

Figuring out how to be a good homemaker and housekeeper became a main way for Minu to deflect her frustrations. Cooking remained a difficult challenge, with many of their meals coming from nearby fast food takeouts, but she was assuming control of other aspects of homemaking. Though she had turned her nose up at housekeeping at first, she now accepted that it was her job. In fact, as she was a very clean person with something of an OCD personality, she lit into housekeeping with a determined passion, fixing up and cleaning her new home, trying to make it constantly spotless.

One day, in the midst of her daily set of chores, she began reflecting on her role as housekeeper, and she realized that doing the housework actually brought her a lot of satisfaction. *I feel like I may be changing,* she thought, while wondering just what that meant since she still felt like the same person she had always been. *Maybe I'm growing up a little.* This idea brought a smile to her face. She had always seen herself as a happy person, and she realized that at heart, she was still mostly happy. And adaptable. Even housework could make her happy! She laughed at that thought. But she also knew that she would be happier if she could find ways to escape the confines of the little apartment.

Chapter 4

New York, New York!

Gradually, things got better and she began to feel herself fitting in. That was helped by her starting to learn more about her adopted city. Though she was unable to partake of New York nearly as much as she wanted—no fancy dining, no Broadway plays, no clubs—she and her husband occasionally got out into the city. One Saturday, they went to world-famous Coney Island, and it was one of the best days she had experienced since arriving. She felt like a world traveler.

She loved these little trips that always raised her appreciation of how independent she had become of her family, and how she had grown. In India she had been Daddy's little girl, but now she was a young woman who was managing her home and getting to know her quiet husband. And she was living in New York City! Every trip out into the city, she felt closer to the idea that this was her true home, where she was finally becoming an adult. The girl who was sheltered and cared for at every step of the way felt like she was finally growing up. It was a thrilling thought.

Though she was becoming increasingly independent, her heart was still very much connected to her parents. She used to write letters to her mom and dad every single day because in those days, international calling was very expensive and connections were not clear. Once, she wrote a letter to her dad asking for his support for her getting a job. This had become an important matter for her as the outings into the city had made her acutely aware that becoming a good homemaker was not enough to still her desire to expand herself and get out into the world more. Yet she remembered her husband saying, when he initially came to see her, that he did not want his wife to work. In the letter to her dad, she explained that she was bored and often alone at home and would like to work. From her letter, her dad could feel how glum and lonely his little girl felt, so he wrote a letter to her husband saying that it would be nice if Minu could work and better herself as she was bored and felt lonely while he was busy at the hospital. He also said in the letter to her husband that she would do as he pleased, as he was very much loved and respected by her parents who had chosen him for their daughter.

Soon, with some trepidation, she asked her husband if she could get a job. To her great pleasure, he said, "Yes." Less than two weeks later, her husband, with his connections and influence, got her a job in the business section at a Coney Island hospital.

She took to the job at once, immediately feeling more

productive and less bored with daily life while her husband was at work. Arguments were fewer as the months slid by, and suddenly her husband was done with his residency. At that point, he had some big decisions to make. Being brilliant, as Minu had come to realize he was, he wanted to specialize in cardiology. With that as his objective, he applied and was awarded a fellowship at Maimonides Hospital in Brooklyn. The money he began receiving was not a great deal more than before, but they were able to move to a somewhat larger apartment near the hospital.

While her husband had his fellowship to occupy many hours in his day, Minu was again starting to get restless. She wanted to do more than the office work in Coney Island. She saw her husband advancing, and she yearned to develop professional skills of her own. Money was tight, and she could not afford higher education in New York, but with her background in economics from the university in India, she decided that the banking industry might be right for her. Maybe she could get in on the ground floor and then start rising, making it a career. After much thought and discussion with her husband, she applied for and completed bank teller training. Quickly after, she found a job as a bank teller at a bank in Manhattan. Her attitude soared. As with the office job, she performed wonderfully. Every day she rode the subway for 45 minutes to her bank, and then another 45 minutes home in the evening. While at work, she loved every second, especially the lunch hour, when she would skip lunch and window shop the myriad stores of Manhattan. She walked on the streets of Manhattan as if she owned the city, so happy and carefree. She felt she belonged there.

Working in the bank also turned out to be a wonderful boost to her home life. After a long day, she would always have stories about her job, her responsibilities, her co-workers, the customers she dealt with, and of course her window shopping. Her husband listened attentively, clearly glad she was now happier due to having the opportunity to expand her life. What neither he nor Minu could know at that point is that working in the bank would soon open up a new opportunity.

One day at her job, one of her customers told her he was a photographer.

"That's must be interesting," she said and began counting out money for a check he had submitted. As the man pocketed the money, she asked, "What do you photograph?"

"I'm mostly a portrait photographer," he replied. "My work has been in a number of magazines. By the way, I would love to take photos of you. You have a beautiful face."

Somewhat embarrassed, Minu said, "Thank you for the compliment, but I really can't."

"Why?" he asked.

"Just can't," Minu said with a smile. "Please have a nice day."

On the way home on the subway that evening, Minu recalled the encounter. She felt flattered by the photographer's offer, but she also thought she would be stepping a little too far out of her comfort zone if she had said she was willing to have her photographs taken for a magazine.

Yet there he was again the next week—the same man, at her station, depositing a check and asking her again to attend a photoshoot. Again her answer was "No."

But he was persistent. As he continued to show up at her window and repeat his invitation, the thought that what he was offering might be her doorway into becoming famous was blossoming in her mind. After his fourth time of asking her the same question, she decided to ask her husband what he thought about the idea.

"Find out more," he said. "Make sure he is a genuine photographer who is who he says he is. If it is all absolutely legitimate, you have my approval."

The next time the man came in with his invitation, she tentatively agreed to the photoshoot but made clear that she first needed proof of his standing as a genuine photographer. "No problem," he said.

The two arranged to meet the next day at lunch time,

and he brought a bushel of proof, including many glossy photographs and the magazines where those same photographs were printed, as well as contracts, letters, degrees, and more. After perusing his evidence, Minu was totally convinced of his legitimacy. "So?" he asked. "Will you do the photoshoot?"

"Yes, I will," Minu replied, "I would love to!"

Before the lunch break was over, arrangements had been made as to when and where the photoshoot would occur, and other details.

The next Saturday, Minu went to her first photoshoot. All the time getting ready and riding to the studio in Brooklyn, her heart was pounding with nerves and excitement. Here, finally, might be the door opening that would lead her to become famous!

On entering the studio, the professionalism of the photographer was apparent to Minu at once. Several lights on rolling stands were arranged around a wide white screen standing off to the side waiting to be rolled into place to produce the perfect lighting. A long rack of fashions that looked to be just her size beckoned to her. On top of the rack sat several hats, while various scarves flowed from a couple of hangers. Near the rack stood a wide three-panel screen behind which she would change, and to one side was a small vanity with chair where she could check her hair and makeup. At the far end of the studio, a door with a small shaded window led into what she guessed was a darkroom where her photos would be developed.

Never having been at a photoshoot before, Minu entered the studio nervously, but the photographer quickly put her at ease with a polished, friendly air. Though she had known the shoot would involve her changing into a number of different clothing sets, she had worn a new emerald green sari-inspired dress especially for the occasion. The photographer remarked at how striking she looked and decided to take the first round of photos of her wearing that dress.

Two hours later, after half a dozen changes and what seemed an endless number of poses and clicking shutters, Minu was exhausted. For the first time, she realized how much emotion, acting, and effort went into trying to produce the perfect look for the camera in a hundred different ways over a short period of time. The photographer seemed pleased with her, declaring several times how easy she was to work with. He asked if she could come back in a couple of weeks. In the meantime, he would develop the photos and begin marketing Minu's image to various clothiers. He seemed confident that she would soon be seeing herself in catalogues. He told her that when she came back, he would have her first portfolio ready so she would be able to market herself if she desired.

On the way home and all the rest of the day and evening, the photoshoot was playing in her mind, if not in the forefront then in the background. She had loved the experience, every moment of it. At one point, the photographer had told her she was a "natural," and she knew it was true. She loved the camera, and she felt the camera loved her.

During the two weeks before the next photoshoot, she learned intimately what the saying "walking on Cloud Nine" meant. Her dreams were laced with cameras, lights, and fashions. She glided through her chores at home and work using one part of her mind—the practical one. The other part—what she felt was her deepest self—embraced the possibilities that seemed to have opened up to her like a figure skater embraces the ice.

At her next photoshoot, the photographer handed her a thick portfolio packet with a dozen 8 x 10 glossies inside. He also handed her a contract for a clothing company that wanted to use her image for some of its fashions. In fact, he said that if she agreed, the entire photoshoot this time would be done with her wearing the company's styles. She read the contract in an elated daze with the photographer explaining parts to her. Once she was sure she understood the ins and outs of the document, she signed it. Business out of the way, she again happily entered the deliciously detailed reality of a photoshoot.

During the next few months, she entered the world of fashion with zeal, learning about modeling agencies, designers, and fashion magazines. It wasn't long before she found herself in the pages of several catalogs. She knew it wasn't fame, but it was a start. She felt it was a good one.

Minu had begun traveling back to India for a few weeks each year to visit her family. On her next trip, she carried her portfolio with her. She told her parents she wanted to take the portfolio to an agency in Delhi to inquire about modeling possibilities. They were enthusiastic and encouraged her to go. When she arrived at the agency, she was greeted warmly and with interest. Not long after she returned to New York, her image appeared in a popular Indian magazine. Now her face was slowly becoming known on two continents.

She had been back in New York only a few months when an Indian actor and director, apparently having learned about her from the magazine in India, contacted her and asked for a meeting. Minu agreed but could not imagine what this man would want to talk to her about.

They met at the Hyatt in Manhattan. The director immediately commented on Minu's beauty and how photogenic she was. Then he wasted no time in telling her that he wanted her to be in a movie he was going to direct. The filming would take place in Bombay, India. She would need to commit to being there for six months while the movie was being shot.

"I can't," Minu replied to the invitation. "I would love to, of course, but I'm married and my life is here, with my husband. If the movie were being filmed here, I could probably do it, but I can't leave my husband for six months. It's impossible."

The meeting left her with mixed feelings. She was certainly flattered by the director's offer. He was providing her an opportunity that might well lead to what she had longed for since a child—true fame—at least in India. But she could not grasp that opportunity. It was simply out of the question.

When she told her husband about the offer—and her refusal—she could see mixed feelings in him too. He was obviously proud of her for having been given the chance to be in a movie, but he was also relieved at her response. Though he had been okay with her modeling so far—even though his parents disapproved—being in a movie would be much more demanding of her time. Even if it were in New York, let alone in India.

When she told them, Minu's parents were happy for their daughter to have been given an opportunity to act in movies, and they started telling their friends and her in-laws. Of course, that did not sit well with her in- laws. On the contrary, his mom felt bad for her son and wondered who he had married.

Though regret for not being able to embrace the opportunity that had suddenly materialized haunted Minu for a few weeks, she bucked herself up with the realization that she still had a modeling career. And that was much better than nothing. Soon her natural resilience and positive attitude washed away most of the regret. She moved on in her mind, deciding that only one thing made sense—to make the very best out of her life as it was.

As the months in New York rolled on, she continued doing photoshoots for various clothiers and advertisers, all of it adding to her portfolio. She now usually worked with makeup artists and hair stylists hired by the various companies, professionals who knew the secrets to showcasing her natural beauty.

Understanding that youthful beauty was the basis of her modeling career, she started learning all she could about nutrition and exercise—the two things that were paramount to being able to retain her looks and vitality for a long period. Then, tired of office work and wanting to pursue all avenues of beauty, and longing to use her knowledge, she quit her job and took on a new one as a health and nutrition guide in a health club.

Over the few years she had lived there, Minu had come to embrace New York City as her true home. Modeling and working in the health club made her feel like she was an integral part of the city, embodying a portion of its energy, excitement, and glamour. New York felt more like home than India. She could not understand why she was—and still is—so connected to New York City. They were poor those days, but she was the happiest. Perhaps there was a past life connection, for those who believe that sort of thing, or it could be that she just did all her growing up there.

It never occurred to her in those exhilarating times that maybe her days in the city were numbered.

Chapter 5

Goodbye, New York

Residency pay was meager and Minu's earnings were not great, so the couple continued to have barely enough money for rent and daily necessities. Yet, while little was left over for entertainment or any kind of night life, Minu was mostly happy now that she felt comfortable in the city and had her modeling endeavors to nurture her dreams. She had little thought about what would happen after her husband completed his fellowship at Maimonides.

Then the day came, and it was time to decide what would be next in their lives, a decision that depended on where her husband would set up his medical practice. The obvious possibilities were nearby, including on Long Island or Staten Island. The idea of leaving the New York City area or the state never occurred to them at first, as they had no family elsewhere in the U.S.

Then one day Minu's husband announced he had received a call from a friend who lived in Fresno, California.

"My friend said there were ample opportunities out there. And the weather is great. He encouraged me to seriously consider setting up my practice out there. What do you think?"

"I don't know anything about California. Besides, I don't want to leave New York. I love the energy here. And after you begin your practice, we'll have more money to do things in the city. Couldn't you set up somewhere nearby, like we talked about?"

"But Minu, just think, no more long, cold winters. We'd have plenty of sunshine throughout the year."

"Winters aren't so bad here. With four seasons, you learn to appreciate each one. Always something new. Different kinds of clothing, different fashions to wear throughout the year."

After several such conversations, Minu hoped she had convinced her husband how much she wanted to stay near New York City. But then he announced he had decided to fly out to visit his California friend for a few days and look for himself at what kind of opportunities were there. Minu stayed in New York, hoping her husband would not like the town or would find that the friend had exaggerated the opportunities there. Her heart dropped when her husband arrived home enthused about what he had learned.

They talked again that night about the possibility of moving, and again Minu resisted as best she could.

"Okay," her husband said. "I understand your qualms. But it's a nice town, and everything is available there. Let's try it for a year. If, after a year, you don't like it there, we will move back to New York."

Minu felt trapped by this offer. It seemed like a reasonable compromise, but she suspected that after a year, her husband's practice might be so well established that it would be difficult to just pick up and move back to New York. Yet she saw no way out, and she reluctantly agreed to the move.

Life was again going to change in a big way for this young woman who was still only a girl in some ways. And once again, she had no clue as to how radically it would change. But she decided that whatever happened, she would accept it. It was her destiny. And according to her mom, everything was destiny.

They sold everything they had, which wasn't much—one used sofa and a hand-me-down table and chairs. Her young sister was visiting her in New York at the time. The three of them packed everything into one car, with their prize possession—a big old TV—in the back seat. Then all three took off on a road trip from New York to California.

As much as Minu regretted leaving New York, it was an exciting time. One thing that made it exciting was that she had found out only a few weeks before that she was pregnant with her first child. Before leaving and while they traveled, she often closed her eyes and dreamed of what it would be like to be a mother. Her heart hoped for a girl, as she yearned to care for, dress, and buy stuffed animals and dolls for a little daughter. She imagined a baby girl dressed up like her own dolls had been when she was a few years younger, in frilly, feminine clothes. She had told few others that she longed for a daughter, as in the Indian community it is customary to want a son as the first child. Even if she said it aloud, the listener would just laugh and not believe her. So, she kept her wishes to herself. But she saw nothing odd in her desire for a daughter, as her parents had raised her differently from many others in her culture. They were more modern in their thinking and never favored one sex over the other. They just wished for their children, of either gender, to be healthy and bring good luck to the parents.

On the way to California, the three travelers felt they were on a grand adventure. They were all so young, and here they were, driving off into the unknown. Minu was glad her younger sister was there to accompany her. They were both children in nature when away from any harshness in life. And they had a special bond, like twins, happy with each other's company, laughing at trivial and silly things.

Finally, after several days of travel, they were almost at their destination, about to start a new phase of life. All the way, she had been envisioning a new environment that would be similar to what the East Coast had been. Now that they were almost there, she began to see how wrong she had been.

Chapter 6

Two Gifts from Heaven

E verywhere Minu looked it was all flat land, mostly huge farms with metal irrigation systems rising from the earth and stretching far across the fields. Off in a hazy distance floated a line of hills that looked so far away they might have been in a different country. They had been in California for several hours and had seen no big cities, no towering buildings. It was all just farm fields, tractors (which she had seen only in Indian movies), the highway, a gas station or two, a few run-down towns, and the ever-present sun above.

"We are almost there," Minu's husband said as they passed a sign indicating only ten miles to the small California city where she had agreed he could set up practice for a year to see how it went.

They exited the freeway, passed a sign indicating the population of the city to be some 30,000 people—really, to Minu, more a town than a city— and were soon driving down a quiet main street that could have been a model for countless other semi-rural, backwater communities in the American West.

Minu was not impressed.

Still, there was nothing to do but make the best of the situation, and she immediately set about doing that. They soon found a house to rent, thankfully roomier than their lodgings in New York had been.

Her husband got to work right away, establishing himself in an independent practice. There were considerable initial expenses in setting up his office, but he went at it with confidence and it quickly became clear that the lean times of his residency were going to be a thing of the past.

In the beginning, there was furniture to purchase and decorating to be done, and Minu was happy to have her sister helping her set up her new home. As long as her sister was there, she had a close companion to keep her company during the days while her husband worked.

Minu couldn't decide whether their new dwelling was actually a home or a kind of prison, especially during the day. The only friends she made in the early months were the wives of a couple of other physicians, but she usually saw them only at occasional evening get-togethers

To get out of the house, she sometimes walked downtown to shop for household goods and see what the local stores had to offer in the way of clothing and home decoration. What a difference from New York City! There, the latest glamorous fashions were always on display in boutique store windows, and a dozen kinds of specialty shops offered an abundance of unique gifts from all over the world. Here, if she found one item that sparked her interest, it was a good shopping day.

Once they had settled into the town, she and her husband started to make more friends. As in New York, their acquaintances were all physicians and their wives, mostly from Punjab and speaking Punjabi. The women were all nonprofessional housewives and very traditional. Again she tried to fit in, but she found the same difficulty as in New York because she was not traditional. She had never worn the Indian traditional sari in India or New York but had always dressed Western. Here in California, at social gatherings the other women dressed traditionally and mocked her Western way of dressing. As a result, she was never totally comfortable at the gatherings. Yet, she loved to be social and so found herself becoming a kind of people pleaser, doing many social events in her home. She had learned on her own how to cook and entertain well and she enjoyed showing her expertise. She reasoned that her social skills were in her genes as her parents had always been very social.

One thing that lifted Minu's spirits was that her kid sister was still there with her, as she, her husband, and her sister were all discovering life together in this new small town. The other thing that kept Minu's spirits up after their move was her pregnancy. She was captivated by the wondrous changes happening to her body and often spent hours thinking and dreaming about what it would be like when she had her baby. She longed for and prayed for a girl.

And what a miraculous day it turned out to be, as they welcomed a beautiful baby girl into their lives! Minu gave thanks to God for answering her prayers and sending down such a perfect tiny angel.

The world changed on that day. Minu was joyful as never before. She forgot about her dislike of the town. It was not relevant. All that was important was a gift from heaven wrapped up in a baby blanket. She was fascinated by the little being she had given birth to. It was as if her own childhood had returned, now in the form of her own daughter.

Once the baby was home, not only Minu, but also her husband and sister got lost in the new world that revolved around the little child. Each of them would stand beside her daughter's crib a dozen times a day, attending to her every move.

Life had suddenly taken on a profound meaning. When Minu herself had been a girl, her natural mothering instinct had been called forth as she played with her cherished dolls. Now, with her childhood returning in a marvelous new way, she had received the gift of a real doll to care for—her own daughter—who she sang to at night, while giving the precious little body gentle massages to express her deep love.

She had come to know what mothers have learned throughout history—that having a child is the greatest joy in the world. Overnight, her thinking had changed. There was no more just Minu. She had become more than herself, with the greatest part of her now being her daughter. Her child had become the center of her universe. All that mattered was her devotion to her baby girl. She determined herself to protect her daughter from all harm and provide her with everything she possibly could.

A few months after her daughter's birth, it was time to

decide whether she and her husband were to stay in California past their one-year agreement. By that time, her husband had established himself in his practice with a growing list of patients. When the subject of staying or returning to New York came up, Minu felt overwhelmed by the argument for staying. She felt she had no choice. First, in Indian culture a woman follows her husband's dreams. Also, she was not professional, so she had no dreams to follow elsewhere. She accepted the decision to stay mostly with equanimity because of the new profound meaning and joy she had found in her daughter.

The child grew under her mother's and father's vigilance and care, and how fast she grew was another aspect of her daughter's life that fascinated Minu. She felt at times that the little girl was growing too fast, the helpless, gurgling baby disappearing into a curious little toddler. Yet, as her daughter grew and began to walk and then talk, at each milestone her mother's pride and happiness were boundless.

Every month for the first year, she celebrated the date of her daughter's birth. Then, a few months after the girl's first annual birthday, Minu discovered that she was again pregnant. The knowledge that her daughter would have a sibling close in age, just as she had as a child, seemed to be excellent evidence of life falling into a harmonious balance.

Again, she sat and dreamed of the new baby, but this time often rocking and singing to her first child as she allowed her mind to carry her to beautiful places. If only the new baby would also be a girl too—that would be perfect. She and her sister had always been very close, and the idea that she might have two daughters who would be as close was a lovely thought. Then they would have each other for life.

Her daughter had just turned two years old when it came time to deliver the new baby. She had no clue whether it was going to be a boy or a girl, as at that time ultrasounds were not done routinely, and the sex of the baby was never the priority. During her pregnancy she sometimes had bad morning sickness. Her daughter was so calm and patient when her mother was feeling ill, never asking for food or a diaper change though she was only a year and some months old. She would just lie beside her mom. Minu's husband was always working, so it was her and her baby girl.

Her older daughter had been born on February 16 and right after, ten days later, another angel from heaven arrived on the 26th. To both parents' delight, it was another little girl. Both parents were overjoyed and thought they were blessed as their older daughter now had a best friend for life.

Another flawless angel sent from heaven, Minu thought as she held the baby in her arms, her joy now doubled. She started calling her newest child *perfection.*

On bringing the new baby home, she explained to her older daughter that she had brought her a new doll for her to love and play with. The older child, still in diapers herself, took to her new sister immediately, treating her with great tenderness. The older daughter was like a little mom to her baby sister. She would carry both her own diaper and her new sister's to her mother when it was time for a diaper change. Whenever she wanted to drink milk, she would say, "Mom, baby wants milk too" in her cutest baby talk. Both her daughters brought back her childhood every day. For

Minu, the biggest miracle in the world was giving birth to and raising these two little angels.

She felt so blessed in her perfect world. Her day was filled with her children's baby talks and giggles. She was reliving her childhood through them. Every second all she wanted was to protect them from any sadness and negative events.

Always a leader and never a follower, Minu decided that the tradition she had started of celebrating her first daughter's birthday each month for the first year should be continued for her second daughter. As she was committed to bringing her girls up in the best way possible, she insisted on a very hands-on way of raising them. It was not the way typically practiced in India, but it was what felt right to her.

During those first few years, she created an ideal world for herself and her children. Every day was a new adventure of playing with them, thinking up activities, and caring for their every need. She was happiest when surrounded by her two daughters.

Two years passed quickly in this totally blissful environment. Too soon, the time arrived for her older daughter to start preschool. It was a very big deal for Minu. Trusting no one else when it came to her children, she had so far been unable to part with either child even for couple of hours.

That day, while trying to remain calm on the outside for the sake of her daughter, Minu was a turmoil of emotions inside. Holding her second child in her arms, she led the older girl, who was dressed in a red corduroy jumpsuit and white shirt, into the preschool room. Immediately, the girl started to cry. Minu, in instant empathy, began crying too.

"Just go," the teacher said to her. "She will be okay once you leave."

Minu bent down and kissed her daughter. "You'll be alright, dear. I will be back soon." She walked outside the classroom and then turned and stood watching until her daughter stopped crying. Then she left. Years later, she remembered that day as one of the hardest days of her life up to that point.

The years continued to pass, and soon it was time for her littlest one to start preschool and her older girl to begin kindergarten. The two schools were on opposite sides of the street. Her little one wanted to go to her sister's school and be with her. When Minu took the little one to preschool, the girl cried hard and kept repeating, "I go to Didi school, I go to Didi school!"

It was another hard day for Minu. She continued often to cry when she sent her kids to school, as her kids would cry leaving her. For several years, she and her children had shared the same small, close, delicious world. Now the children's worlds had begun slowly expanding into new areas, and it felt to Minu as if that were leaving holes in her own world. She began to wonder whether, in the future, she would ever be able to part from them and see them go away to school.

But she didn't allow those thoughts and feelings to persist. She still had too much pleasurable work to do in raising her kids. She continued to hold them close to her and loved dressing them up as her precious little angels, as if they were part of her. But she also saw the importance of giving her girls the best experiences in the world to help them be well rounded, so she introduced both daughters to various activities. She was the epitome of the dedicated mom who took her children to swimming lessons, dance lessons, and tennis lessons. As much as she loved to hold them close to her, a main part of her philosophy in raising her children was to help them grow up to be strong and independent.

The girls were athletes from an early age. In winter, Minu often took them snowboarding and skiing at China Peak, about two hours away. When they were eight and ten years old, she enlisted a private ski instructor for lessons. Not totally trusting the instructor with her beloved girls, Minu couldn't stop herself from tagging along behind as he gave his lessons. While not a skilled skier herself in those days, she managed to keep her distance, not wanting to upset the instructor with her wary behavior, like a mother lion protecting her cubs.

When the girls got older, they wanted to learn snowboarding, so Minu once again learned with her daughters as she took them to the snow and enjoyed snowboarding with them.

Minu's world was her two angel daughters, and she wanted to raise them outside the box. She introduced them to various activities, and they could choose and excel at what they liked. She enrolled them in an all-year competitive swim team and took them to practices. While the girls were swimming, instead of hanging around the poolside, she took up jogging. While her girls swam, she ran on the track and got her exercise.

She also introduced them to horseback riding, roller skating, and ice skating. At the same time, she became quite athletic herself. She basically grew up with her daughters as she learned all the sports she introduced them to. She even took swimming and diving lessons. It was as if she were going through her childhood again, but better, as she shared and enjoyed various activities along with her precious daughters.

Happily, Minu still plays tennis, snowboards, and jogs five miles five times a week. She has found joy in running, learning you can run anywhere if you have the proper shoes. She does all her thinking and decision making while running, as she feels free when she runs. She always was a Type A personality, with high energy, and she always loved that fact about herself as she got a lot accomplished being that way.

When her girls were junior high age, she thought she would teach them some baking. All the ingredients to prepare some cookies or cake were set out on the counter, and then an egg rolled off and onto the floor. Never known for her patience, Minu announced that the lesson was over. Her next thought was, *Why worry? They will do so well in life, they will be able to hire a cook.*

As her daughters grew, it became time to start preparing them for learning to drive. The older girl first took the steering wheel at 13, not on the highway, but in the vacant fields behind the house. With her daughter in the driver's seat, Minu sat on the console in the middle with her foot on the gas and within reach of the brake to let the girl get an early feel for what it's like to steer a car. Lessons progressed slowly and safely.

A year or two later, it was time for her younger daughter to start learning. Because in an earlier year the girl had been afraid to drive a go cart, Minu was uncertain about how well she would adjust to steering a car. But she took to the lesson enthusiastically. For both girls, when it came time for them to learn real driving, they did an excellent job. Years later they both would show how their early lessons had paid off by enjoying several occasions when they had the opportunity to drive race cars at a track.

As they grew, it quickly became clear that the two girls had different personalities. They both were driven to be number one. As a result, they were at times hard on themselves, though there was no pressure from their parents. They were both tennis players, but they displayed different reactions when they did not do well according to their expectations. When the older one did not win, she would walk away from tennis court with a sad and disappointed look. The younger one would also be disappointed, but she was more resilient and handled losses at the game better. Aside from these different reactions, they both strived to be the best in everything from a very early age. Both daughters were always focused and always knew what they wanted to achieve in their lives. They never took any year off. They had laser vision.

Minu realized that each of her daughters reflected personality characteristics of both herself and her husband. She also understood that though quite different, the two personalities complemented each other, which the girls demonstrated by remaining close throughout their childhood and beyond. They became each other's strength as life began to unfold. Minu felt she was blessed that her daughters would always have each other's back and never be alone in the world. She envisioned them as being real soul mates.

Chapter 7

Away to Boarding School

A gain, the years passed too quickly, and another crossroads came into sight as it was nearly time for Minu's older daughter to enroll in high school.

Minu has had big dreams for her daughters, as she had had for herself, and in her opinion, the best base for fulfilling those dreams was not the town's public high school. For one thing, her daughters were gentle and polite, while the kids in the public high school tended to be rowdy and misbehaved. She also felt that the academic standards in the public school were not high enough. Having gone to university and excelled in her studies, she had an appreciation for quality in education. And both her daughters were brilliant. Throughout grade school they had been excellent students with high grades. They deserved the best education they could obtain. And that could be had at an excellent boarding school.

Her husband viewed the matter differently. He believed that children who were hardworking and focused could achieve anything whether from a small school or not. She realized that maybe he was right for some kids, but she argued that the school and environment were important too, and to give a child the very best chance at success, those elements had to be right.

Discussion about high school continued. It was a huge step and a big decision. What made the matter even more difficult for Minu was that she found it so hard to stay even a day away from her daughters, yet here she was arguing for the possibility of sending their oldest off to boarding school. But she still could not see her children going to a public high school. Torn between wanting to hold on to her daughter and her daughter's higher education, she could not be selfish. Her daughters deserved the best every step of the way, and she believed strongly that good secondary schooling is the solid foundation for higher education, as good education and schooling stays with you throughout life.

Her husband took a lot of convincing, but they finally decided to send their older child to a well-regarded boarding high school in Los Angeles.

Her daughter was only 13. On the day of leaving her daughter at the boarding school, Minu once again felt weak in her knees. Emotions were high on the day of parting, but on the way home, she was able to relieve her sadness somewhat by telling herself that she had managed to put her child's future first.

At home, she thanked God that she still had her younger

daughter there for another two years. But she could see that her little one missed her sister being there.

She stayed in close communication with her older daughter and was pleased to learn she was adapting fairly quickly to the high school and was having success in her classes. One good thing about the boarding school was that it was only a three-hour drive to get there. That made it easy for her to get into the habit of driving down twice a week to watch her daughter swim or play tennis. Also, every weekend she, and at times her husband, drove down to be with their daughter.

All the visits made the time fly, and it wasn't long before two years had passed and it was time for her little one to go to high school, too. There was never any doubt that she would join her sister at the boarding school. Her younger daughter was excited to enroll, as she would be with her sister.

Once both girls were gone to boarding school, Minu became very sad. The house was empty. No girls coming home in the afternoon to share their day and to fix dinner for. No husband at home, as he was always busy working to provide the very best for the family.

She remembered what her mom had always said: You must learn to live your own life and not try to live it through your children. Well, maybe in India that was possible, as they had maids and nannies to help raise the children. There, parents had their own life and routine. They were around but not hovering over the children. But for Minu, who had made it her singular job to care for her daughters herself from the beginning, it seemed an impossible thing to do.

She could not see beyond her daughters. Her perfections.

Chapter 8

Song Lyrics

While in boarding high school in Los Angeles, Minu's older daughter spent some of her free time writing songs. Minu thought the song lyrics were very good and provided an opportunity to understand her child better. Eventually, her older daughter gathered a collection of songs, and Minu encouraged her to get them published. Here, she shares some of the songs her older daughter wrote as a teenager.

Songs Written by Minu's Older Daughter

REGRET

Remembering the past retract
I'd take the words back
I'd do things differently React
I would listen patiently.

ADRENALINE

I feel it runs through my body
Pervading through every vein
I sense my body lifting
I'm barely staying same
My heart starts to pound
My body begins to shake
Can hardly keep my feet on the ground
Seems like anything I can break

STRETCH MY MIND

Stretch my mind
Expand it
Teach me more things, don't leave me behind.

Help me help those
Who have been made incapable to think for
themselves
See that, for others they've no reason to pose.

Show them there is no reason to quit
Into the issues they should delve
Push what you think is right
Push what for a peaceful shift
Go help, get off your ass just don't sit

With a united group
Have no fear of being dismissed

Stand strong, you won't be avoided forever.
Like cattle you won't be coupled … up.
Just don't resist
Give it in your basic good
Change those who are racist
Manage to give the hungry food.

Stretch your mind
Open your eyes and see the possibilities
Those who wear shielded from seeing when
they had your thoughts confined.
See the grief your lack of action has caused
Get into gear
Make those controlling tux fear
Fear those whose mind, minds they thought
they paused.

STRENGTH

I stand here as strong as glass
Streaked with miniature cracks
One pane insane
The nocturnal tongue we speak in

Our nocturnal tongue

I have no heart & I don't want yours

I have no heart & you're no lover of mine

I have lost myself to this beat:
Our nocturnal tongue.
The disturbingly comfortable rhythm we have
reached
Everything I never wanted

Everything I don't care for

And I have surrendered myself to it.

TWENTY-ONE

You are growing up.
Gotta shape up.
Leave behind all your fuck ups.
No extra privileges.
Still can't drink in bars.
If you do you know it's against the law.

But, you're heading Into your prime
Persevere
It's no time to lay down and die.

Getting older.
Maybe bolder.
No longer a teenager.

"Act your age."

You will hear over and over.

One more year.
And you can buy your own beer.
Until then
Settle for what you get.
Grow up
Shape up
Fuck up
Make up
Show up
Shut up
Suck it up.
You're almost 21.

You're growing up

Whoo A

Running outta luck I've got to say, 20.
Seems like it'd suck.

EMOTIONALLY DETACHED

Didn't scratch my surface
Didn't even nick my skin
You disillusioned yourself
And thought I let you in.
All our night together
Left you with no hints
As to who I am
As to why I let you near.

Misfit

The nocturnal tongue we speaking in

Gave me no due as to why you,

Failed to realize I'm the opposite of what you think

Maybe the opposite of what you want.

My emotions are not yours, not for you
I've no heart and I don't want yours
I've no heart you are no lover of mine

Take it back all that you said
Take it back all that you did
Tried so hard, but you failed
You left me I didn't shed a tear.

I lost nothing
You took nothing
None of me with you.

MIND

Pounding, drilling, molding
My mind about to explore
They won't let me think
Let me be on my own.

The sounds hammers on the right, push me to left
I am strongly advised, "Away the commotion"
I proceed, unaware of the awaiting theft, thinking
"They know best"
The nails, unyielding tools of theirs
Hinder me from reentering to where I came
My direction is increasingly limited with each forced nail.

Forced into the walls of creativity
My mind's playground, smaller with each piece of advice I follow
They tell me avoidance and apathy equals calmness and happiness
Why then is my mind trembling more?
My soul feeling violated?

Despite my tendency to doubt my "choice" of movement
I follow, maybe that next step, from my last
Maybe then I will feel the way they tell me I will.
Step turns into a mile
The farther I go, the less I see
I strain my neck right & left to see what I left behind
Each inch my feet take forward

Removes slowly my ability to look around for
myself.
I depend on what they tell me, surrounds
more and more.
The nails dig through bones
Causing me to question more
Yet I become more determined that it's next
step
Ultimate fulfillment will follow this pain
They said it would,
Who am I to say they're wrong.
I can't see and still I follow
They could be leading me to hell. And I would
not know.
I trust them more than myself. For reasons
unknown
I doubt yet still follow
Simply cuz they told me to.

ATHEIST

Not sure if there is a God
Sometimes I think religion is just a fraud.
Pagan
There is no savior
Everything is a result of our behavior.
This is not how it was meant to be
Your religion has blinded you
Close-minded you
For yourself you're unable to see.

"God willing"

You're made to think you can only help by praying You forgot you have ability to change everything Just stop kneeling and stand on your two feet.

Theories, you blindly accept
Without putting them to the test
Ignorant opinions
That's why the world is such a mess.
But I won't write you off

Just because you believe in something different than me.
I just wish you would open your eyes
Open your eyes and see.

Question what you're taught

Don't just talk the talk
After you think, if you still believe
Count on nothing but respect for me.
And if you lose your faith
You won't burn in hell

Regardless of what they say

But no longer will your soul be for sale.

Back to University

With both daughters in boarding school, the structure that had shaped Minu's life for the last 15 years was mostly gone. Of course, there were the visits to the boarding school, and the girls were back home during the summers, but there were many lonely, empty days. She felt lost, not knowing what to do with herself.

After a lot of thought, she decided that it was time she struck out to learn and do something new. She decided to go back to school to study science and eventually try to enter a physician assistant program. That was her husband's recommendation as he, being a physician, found his profession very rewarding.

She debated the decision in her head for a while as she had never had science in high school, and she was more interested in law. She first inquired about being a lawyer.

But going to small school in Fresno did not sit well with her. She wanted to be a graduate from a good standard university.

There were no good reputable schools nearby, but she knew there was a good medical school not too far away.

She also recalled her father's desire that she should be a doctor. She remembered how disappointed her dad was when she had attended a cosmetologist school that was within walking distance of her house. But she had only attended that school to keep herself busy, as in the small town there was nothing else to do.

She finally decided to become a physician assistant.

After taking classes for a few years in a local community college, she applied to enter the University of California at Davis physician assistant program. By God's grace, she was accepted immediately, as if it was meant to be. Though she had never been dedicated to science before and had always wanted to be a model or a movie star, she reasoned that maybe God wanted her to be a healer.

She worked hard at the university and graduated in the top ten percentile. Soon after, she obtained a position as a physician assistant at a medical practice near her home. Though she did well in the position, it seemed to her that she had not accomplished enough. She decided to go for a Master's degree in Emergency Medicine and did just that.

It was no coincidence that at this time, her older daughter had graduated from the boarding school and entered a university in a pre-med program. This fact spurred Minu on in her own efforts, as she believed in the importance of setting a good example for her precious daughters, convinced that children learn more by seeing and modeling than by being told.

It made her happy to know that their daughters had grown up seeing how hard both of their parents worked. The girls also realized that their parents' lives began and ended with their daughters. The result was two beautiful young women who had grown to be humble and to have gentle, caring hearts of gold, while at the same time they were also focused on achieving something substantial in their lives.

Her daughters always encouraged her to be in school and achieve whatever her heart desired. Her little angels were repeating the same thing she used to tell them. When Minu would say she was too old to go back to school, her precious daughters would say, "No Mom, you can do it." She was raising her daughters, but she was also learning from them. At every step of life she felt grateful for her children.

Chapter 10

Making Minu Proud

Today, Minu's children are perfect young adults with impressive accomplishments. They make their parents intensely proud. Both learned from their parents that nothing comes easy: hard work is required for making significant achievements. They also learned they must have dreams to work for and must set goals for themselves.

Today, they are successful because they worked hard and went after their dreams. The older daughter has become a thriving interventional cardiologist in New York City. The younger daughter is a well accomplished entertainment attorney. She is one of the youngest partners in her firm and has dual licenses for California and New York.

Both young women also take time to enjoy life, being active socially and in sports. They still delight in snowboarding and playing tennis.

When the girls moved away from home to college and

then into their respective professions, Minu kept in close touch with them, often calling, writing letters, and sending e-mails. She continued to provide her daughters with life guidance as she had throughout their childhood. A message from May 9, 2015 expresses her love for her daughters and captures her motherly wisdom:

Dear Daughters,

My beautiful daughters, love of my life. You girls made me a mother and my whole life changed and had a new meaning to it. You both are part of me, and always will be my little girls. Once you become a mother you earn a right to worry, care and love your kids.

What advice can I give to my beautiful level-headed girls?

My own life has taught me not to be a people pleaser, as in reality people will never be happy, they will always find faults in you and be judgmental. So just please yourself.

Always stand tall, and learn to roll with the punches of life. Nothing stays forever. Always be grounded.

If you don't know what to do in a difficult situation, the best thing is not to do anything at all, as life has a way of working itself out.

Sometimes too much loving and too much caring is interpreted as controlling. So learn early on everything you do in life, there is absolutely no need to go overboard. Remember that, as in the end, only you will be miserable.

Lose toxic and negative people around you, as they will bring you down. Always trust your instinct as it's always right.

Life is sooooo beautiful, cherish it, experience good things, and above all live outside the box.

Whatever you are doing, don't let the past move your mind, don't let the future disturb you. Because the past is no more, and the future is not yet, so live in the present.

Always always be there for each other. Understand each other. You both complement each other. Hand in hand live your life and share with each other your ups and downs. You both have a little bit of your mom in you— loving each is loving me.

You both are the most precious gift to each other and me. Love forever till eternity

Minu sees her two daughters as wonderful models for today's women, who she is convinced can achieve as high as they can dream.

At the time of this writing, both young women are well established in their profession. Now Minu envisions the next phase of their lives.

She notes how times have changed. There are no arranged marriages anymore. And she fully supports that. She never would encourage her daughters to have an arranged marriage or to marry in the same culture. She believes all cultures are pretty similar and that every culture has its own traditions and rituals. Every religion and culture teaches us the same principles.

Her view on marriage is that spouses should be equal partners and should have mutual respect. Partners should equally support each other's dreams.

Chapter 11

Empty Nest Syndrome

With her two daughters gone to make their own ways in life, Minu began experiencing empty nest syndrome—the feelings of sadness and loss some parents undergo when the last child leaves the family home. It affects mostly women, as they have been the main caretakers and nurturers of children over the centuries. Parents with empty nest syndrome experience a deep void in their lives, and they often feel a little lost. They may also struggle to allow their adult children to have autonomy, as it's hard for them to let go.

Minu reflects that parents sometimes look ahead to their golden years and envision themselves surrounded by loving grandchildren, but it doesn't always happen that way. At least, not right away. The vision, she says, neglects another fundamental truth: people change. If we rely on other people for our happiness, we may be disappointed. We all must learn to live alone, emotionally and physically. But that is easier said than done.

Minu was surprised by the depth of her sadness. She always encouraged her depressed patients to practice positive thinking and focus on themselves. She herself was never a needy or depressed person; and in fact, she hates that word, "depression," as she believes life is a beautiful gift that we must enjoy. Yet, her personal experience in reaction to her younger daughter moving away was unexpected.

At first, there was a period of transition. With her older daughter living far from home in New York City, the younger one lived in Beverly hills, not too far away, so she was able to visit her twice a month and spend the weekend there in the family condo Minu and her husband had bought for her. The family condo was purchased to allow the entire family of four to get together and enjoy each other's company. Her daughter from New York would fly in, while she and her husband would drive from their small town. The condo was bought just because her younger daughter was there; otherwise, there was no reason to buy a condo there, as her heart always wanted to move back to New York City. She and her husband even decided to build a house in Beverly Hills primarily because her younger daughter was there, while they worked in California's Central Valley (she still can't figure it out why after 36 years, her mind still questioning).

Though they had the family condo, and her younger daughter lived there just a few hours away, she had raised her daughters to be very independent and live the life that she could not. That included wanting them to have their own places, which they could call theirs, not mom and dad's. When both daughters started doing well, she began telling them to invest in real estate. She never imagined that what she put in motion for the betterment of her daughters would emotionally be hard on her.

Following Minu's advice, her younger daughter bought a beautiful condo for herself. Minu was part of the process at every step and was excited for her. But the day her daughter moved out and she came back to the family condo, she cried herself to sleep as she missed her little girl so much.

She would go in her room, stand there, and wonder, what is life? Kids are yours for a very short time.

She was happy her daughter had accomplished so much and could afford a gorgeous place for herself. She had always wanted that for them, but the empty nest syndrome and being alone from her kids and husband finally hit her hard. She is attached to her kids, but she was very surprised at the reaction she had—crying like a baby.

It took a while, but after a year she has adjusted well. She still goes to spend the night at her baby's place. She loves saying that and feels so proud and happy. She wants her children happy whether they are near or far. During that year, she has also joined a country club, made new friends, and started doing yoga. As well, she is thinking of opening a walk-in clinic in her town, as she has always been a doer and not a stay-at-home person.

She still wants to leave this world with shoes on and setting a good example for her children.

Life is ever changing, she says, and she does not want a stagnant life. Now her older daughter has bought her own place in New York, and Minu and the rest of the family are all soooo excited for her. As a mother, she is happy that her daughters are established and never will have a feeling of insecurity in their lives. She feels blessed and grateful to God. She always misses her kids, but she is delighted to see them happy and settled.

Now she will rediscover herself.

Chapter 12

Life as a Physician Assistant

Given that she lived in a small town away from the fashion and entertainment industries, Minu considered becoming a physician assistant to be her best option. She told herself that it was either that or go milk the cows. She says that of course, there is nothing wrong with the latter if one likes doing that. However, she decided on the other option.

She entered the physician assistant program at UC Davis having already obtained some education in cardiology. After finishing that program, she wanted, as always, still more education. Accordingly, she then completed the Master's degree in Emergency Medicine. Following that, she took a job working in family practice and part-time in cardiology.

Physician assistants (PAs) examine patients, prescribe medicine, and order diagnostic tests. In most cases, they work under the supervision of a physician or surgeon, but they can work more independently in some states, rural areas, and inner-city areas, consulting with physicians only when they need help with cases. In many instances, physician assistants counsel patients and their families regarding treatments and patient management plans. They may also take on managerial duties in which they supervise nurses, aides, and other office personnel, while managing the office or clinic. They have a huge responsibility and a job that requires utmost perfection.

Working as a physician assistant started off great for Minu. She loved helping people and liked being their health advocate. She was adored by her patients. The physician she worked with was great, and she was given full freedom to make diagnoses and provide treatment.

For ten years she was very happy, but then things begun to shift. The office was now being managed by the physician's family member and she felt she was no longer respected there. Every day she started to dread going to work. It was her patients that kept her going for a few more years. Small towns are often full of patients with drug addiction, and though she would not write any prescriptions for narcotics, she did follow her physician's orders on refills. But she always felt uneasy doing so.

She also made herself very well informed on women's health and enjoyed empowering them on their health issues. She felt that if patients were well informed, they would do better. With that in mind, she started to write a blog on women's health empowerment.

As the years progressed, she felt that being a physician assistant was demeaning to her. She felt she worked very hard but was not appreciated. Especially in a small town with narrow thinking, a physician assistant was not given due respect. Maybe her feelings were partly because she always was a high achiever and could not come to terms with being at a middle level.

When she began not being respected at the office, her going to work started getting very stressful. The demographics of the patients changed, which made it impossible to practice real medicine. Finally, after 16 years of being a dedicated underpaid physician, she called it quits from family practice. Multiple factors played a role in leaving an office that felt like a second home.

She then added more days in cardiology and loved it. No writing of narcotics was the main attraction, and she loves the interactions with patients. But her heart now wishes she was either a cardiologist or not in medicine at all.

Health

Life after 50 has not always been easy for Minu. She began to have persistent back pain that finally necessitated an operation. The back surgery was hard. She felt blessed that at the time of the surgery, both her daughters were with her, her older daughter having flown in from New York. Her husband took that weekend off.

She woke up with more pain but refused to take narcotics. In her job as an underpaid physician's assistant she had seen too many people become addicted to pain relievers, often after minor surgeries. Her kids stayed with her for several days and took good care of her. She wondered at the fact that time had flown so fast that now her daughters were acting like her mother. Her real mother in India called after the surgery and asked for a current photograph of Minu. She wanted to give it to pundits so they could remove the evil eye she believed was on her daughter.

After her older daughter flew back to her job in New York, Minu was able to spend recovery time with her youngest one in Los Angeles. This was emotionally very good for her as she was having a difficult time dealing with the pain and discomfort and staying positive. Both morning and afternoon, she would see her daughter's angel face as she made sure her mother followed her doctor's instructions. She fell into a healthy routine while staying with her daughter. She would go for physical therapy during the day and in the evening have a nice walk. She also made a few new friends who came to visit her.

After six weeks, it was time to return to her home and husband. It wasn't long before loneliness and boredom started consuming her. With her husband working long hours, there seemed nothing to do, no place interesting or pleasant to walk, nothing to stimulate her. She wished she had something to be excited about in life, something that could give each day greater meaning.

Those days of wandering around her usually empty house as she healed from her back surgery helped Minu realize there was much more to learn and experience, and she was not meant to live in a box. After finally healing from the surgery, she went back to work part time, deciding that otherwise she would lose her mind.

Partly as a result of her health problems, she started feeling the older someone gets, the faster life passes them by and the less control they have over what life brings. She began understanding why people seek and embrace religion, realizing everyone is headed in the same direction and wants to understand what their life means. As a result, her thoughts turned increasingly to spiritual matters, an area she had mostly avoided in younger years.

This change in her frame of mind was sometimes reflected in her actions. One incident was triggered by her chronic back trouble. At work one day, an office assistant, a Hispanic girl, noticed that Minu was in pain and remarked, "Why don't you go to the healer? With her prayers, she will cleanse you and you will feel much better."

At home, she contemplated the girl's words. She knew that virtually all cultures have spiritual healing traditions that are often out of the mainstream. In Hindu culture, one widespread belief is that a person can be the focus of an "evil eye" that causes suffering. To counteract and protect against the evil eye, various prayers can be offered by high officials of the temple.

She had often argued with her religious mother against this kind of thinking, yet now she decided to investigate further on the Internet. She was shocked to learn how many kinds of supposed spiritual healers, practitioners, and advisors she was able to find easily—people practicing black magic, tarot readers, mediums, channelers, and others.

Minu had always prided herself on her practicality when it came to getting along in the world, and she had no real evidence the healer the assistant had mentioned was gifted. She also knew it was a business. Yet, her recent musings about spirituality and the nagging fact of her chronic pain decided her on visiting the healer.

Nervous, skeptical, and not feeling quite herself, she entered the room, sat, and told the woman about her pain and being referred by someone. "I'm a physician assistant and I believe in science and facts, but I'm willing to see if you can help me."

The woman could sense that Minu was skeptical. "If you want to leave, you can," she said.

"No. I am so tired of the pain. It is consuming my life. I am here for you to heal me."

The woman proceeded to perform her prayers. When she was done, she said that Minu could come again if she wished.

When Minu walked out of the house, the pain was still there, but she felt calmer, as if the meeting had lifted some weight off her emotionally. She did not go back, but the incident seemed to encourage, not dampen, her thoughts about spirituality.

At home, she kept thinking, *Is this what life is all about when your children are grown? This emptiness?* She was not depressed exactly, as she loved life and was not the kind to become depressed. But she longed for a job she was passionate about. If she had to do medicine, she wished she could do it as a physician, not a physician assistant, so she could be more respected in her profession.

She regarded her husband, who was very happy and at ease where they were. Why couldn't she be like that? Why couldn't she be contented here? But she had never really liked the town and had always felt stuck here. It was only caring for her daughters as they grew that had made the town livable for her.

She often wondered what was wrong with her. Was she born to be just a side wing? She thought: *People say that when kids grow up you are born again and can follow your dream. But in reality that is bullshit, as every dream has an expiration date. What one can do in their 20s can't be done in their 50s. Maybe sometimes you can manufacture new dreams, but to follow them there may also be a high price to pay, a price that could have been paid more easily 20 or 30 years ago.*

She knew her husband was a great guy, but she realized that they had never seen or thought about the world in the same way. There had often been a huge understanding gap that had been frustrating. But because their marriage had a solid foundation, they had made it work. For her part, she knew she had worked at it hard, as she loved him and didn't know any better.

Still, she remained frustrated and lost, as she conversed with herself, her mind seeking an answer. *Maybe all my dreams when I was a girl were just fantasies,* she thought. *Reality is different than fantasy. And I guess I never learned the art of living and how to be happy and contented whatever the circumstances. Seems like I want it all. But then again, what's wrong with that?*

In her spiritual thinking, she decided that there definitely is a supreme power. Though we do not see it, it is all around us like the air we breathe but cannot detect visually. But her certainty did little to help her come to terms with her feeling untethered, without clear guidance for her life.

She remembered her mother, who was always a symbol of strength. Her mother believed deeply in destiny. She always said, "Nothing happens before its time has come. So always be contented and happy."

Though she had pondered that philosophy many times, she still found it hard to accept.

I guess I still have a lot to learn, she concluded tentatively. She then continued dealing with the question of what would be next.

Chapter 14

What Next?

Though Minu's return to work helped in the short term, she continued wondering about her life purpose. She often felt driven to accomplish more in her lifetime. But what? She scoured her childhood and younger life for clues. She remembered people telling her parents that their daughter was super intelligent. Her accomplishments so far had shown her that both sides of her brain were very active. On the one hand, she was artistic and creative, but at the same time she thought scientifically and logically—the perfect combination.

Yet, what to do next still escaped her. As she analyzed the events in her life, she realized that many of the things she had tried to change just did not happen. Roads she could have traveled down were blocked and their opportunities dissolved. She began to appreciate more her mother's perspective on fate. Perhaps whatever was meant to happen for her would happen. If she was not happy with her town and could not mentally accept and embrace it, then maybe that too was meant to be. Perhaps there was some lesson there she was supposed to learn.

A poem she once wrote reverberated in her mind:

Set me free,

Break the chain of love.

I truly am a free-spirited person.

At times she felt she was not following the advice she had given her girls about not living in the past. She found herself frequently looking at her children's photo album and remembering days long gone. With misty eyes, feeling like the past was a dream, she sat and wondered where life had gone.

On Mother's Day 2017, both daughters were together in New York. Feeling that life is too short, Minu decided it was time to pass her father's ring on to her children. It was the ring she had worn in a necklace for more than a decade after her father's death. She had a jeweler cut the ring in half and make the two halves into pendants, which she sent to her daughters along with a written letter:

> *My amazing daughters, who are my priceless gift from God,*
>
> *This Mother's Day, you both are together. I am going to hand over my favorite possession— my Dad's, your Nana's, ring. I wore it for a decade after he left me.*
>
> *You both are part of my heart and complete me.*
>
> *Let this ring be a symbol of you both always being connected and completing each other. Always be each other's strength. I am thankful you both have different personalities as one needs a different thought process in life than one's own.*
>
> *I got the ring made into pendants, so you both have one half.*

You both are perfection. I really don't think you know how special and wonderful you both are. People surrounded by you are lucky. You are the light for everyone around, and I am soooo proud to be your mother.

Love always

Minu felt blessed when both daughters expressed their happiness and gratitude at receiving their mother's present.

Catharsis

ater in 2017, Minu decided to set down, in writing, her dissatisfaction with the town she had been living in for most of her adult life. She felt that getting her feelings out would serve as a kind of catharsis. She titled her declaration,

My Thoughts.

How do you cope with living in an area you H-A-T-E?!?

Does anyone else hate where they live? I hate it here so much I always feel I am dying inside. I get anxiety, feel frustrated much of the time. Yet I cannot move, as my husband likes it here. He is happy and contented. I am trapped.

I moved from New York City to Hanford, California. I have been living here for 31 years.

I am not happy here and never was. I struggle every day, now more than ever. Unhappiness follows me like a slug trail. I still hate it. I can truly say I hate it here with every core of my being.

The town represents everything I hate. My soul burns in this sizzling heat. I am a city person, I love tall buildings, cement, and asphalt, all surrounded by greenery. I love New York. No city is like New York with its high energy.

In this town, it's as if life is passing me by. I am not living it. This town is like a hideout from the entire world. It's where hopes and dreams are buried. I hope this town does not kill me before my time. I am struggling every day to be happy. It has been a long 31 years.

The town has no decent restaurants, gym, or shopping places. I like to be outdoors but there are few inviting places outside. I love my house, and that's all.

This is a rural area, with no good education, no sophistication. People are rude here. It is a low socioeconomic area, full of third-world diseases. It seems half the town is addicted to drugs and the pregnancy rate is the highest in the nation. People apparently have nothing else to do except have sex and spread STDs.

I've really tried to like it here and I've tried really hard to fit in. But for 31 years, I've disliked the climate here, the attitude of the people, the remoteness, and on and on I could go.

Maybe I am wrong in how I perceive myself as I often think I may have a character flaw I'm not aware of. But I think I'm a fun person who tries to be positive most of the time. I believe I am a very loyal, honest, encouraging, and giving person. I know I have cared too deeply sometimes, and about everyone.

With that said, I was really happy where we lived last, in New York City. Things weren't perfect, but I felt like I fit in. I knew where I was, knew and appreciated everything in my neighborhood, from a little grocery store around the corner to the laundromat. I felt I had a purpose there. I wanted to achieve something. We had no money, but we were happy. Now we have the money but I am not happy.

Is God teaching me something? Is it all destiny? Am I going to die in Hanford? I wonder.

I really do try to see the best in things, but I constantly have feelings of hating it here and of being suffocated.

I am humbly blessed with an awesome husband, healthy intelligent children, a beautiful home, and many other blessings.

But as hard as I try, I cannot shake these feelings. All is destiny, I believe. Or is it?

Do you think it matters where you live? Does the quality of your life change whether you live in place A or place B? Or will a person who is happy in A also be happy in B, while an unhappy person will be unhappy in both?

Do you think there are certain places that "match" us, and therefore create an environment where we feel at home and happy? Or do you think people will still be the same people no matter where they go?

Too much is unknown.

I guess I will just go with flow. I will adopt five rules that are supposed to promote lasting joy:

Honesty is the best policy. Give up toxic people.

Let it go.

Trust your gut.

Know that you are more powerful than you think.

Growing

After 50, Minu realized that she was changing. Unlike in earlier years, she did not let others make her feel incompetent. She understood that though she might not be good at certain things, she was excellent at others.

She knew there was a time when she had been too much of a people pleaser, but she no longer felt the need to fit others' ideas of who or what she should be. She felt, more than ever, comfortable in her own skin.

She walked away from people who did not value her. Though they might not acknowledge her worth, it was not worth her time to confront them about it. Let them believe what they wanted. She knew her worth.

She was now more centered within herself. She used to speed on the freeway, wanting to always be in front. Now she remained calm and let the other cars and other people pass her by. Why hurry? Enjoy the ride.

She was learning not to be embarrassed by her emotions. She understood that it was her emotions that made her human. She understood herself to be, after 50, a little more emotional and at times more sensitive.

She now demanded what was due to her. She would not accept injustice. She felt that accepting injustice was almost as bad as doing injustice.

She was learning to live each day as if it were her last, to do what made her happy each day. She realized that she, no one else, was responsible for her own happiness, and she owed it to herself.

Yes, she was changing. She now saw herself and the world more through the lens of her mother's thought processes. Realizing that life is too short, she felt that maybe our life path is already written and what happens, happens for reasons that are at times unknown to us.

She felt that sometimes maybe God had been saving her from her own self.

As she got older, she was beginning to accept living in two very different kinds of place, to appreciate both urban and small town living. What did it matter whether she was in California or New York, a big or a small town?

Because wherever she lived, she always had a routine, Minu's routine.

As time passed by, her husband began to support her more and more. He realized that she is not a small-town person and she thrives in the city. She comes alive there.

Their younger daughter bought a place in West Hollywood, and so she and her husband decided to put their roots in Beverly Hills. This way, family could be together. It was also more convenient for her older daughter to fly from New York City to Los Angeles to visit them all.

Minu was beginning to think that maybe God always had a plan for her and that He wanted her to experience both rural and urban life, as they are two different cultures. Maybe doing so is a way to live outside the box and to experience all on the journey of life.

Chapter 17

Relationships

An acquaintance of Minu, an Indian woman, who later became a close friend. One afternoon, her friend started talking about her Indian in-laws over cup of coffee, and Minu was struck by what her story revealed about how some Indian women are still not respected by their in-laws.

Her friend told Minu that her in-laws never liked her or her family from day one. She really did not understand why, as time went by, she could not somehow win her in- laws' hearts. She confessed that it remained an enigma to her, but that she had learned not to dwell on it.

The friend continued, saying that her marriage had few obstacles in the beginning, as her husband did not defend her against her in-laws. In fact, She felt that, he always defended them. She said that whenever her in-laws came to her house, she respected them from the bottom of her heart and was very caring towards them.

They would leave happy; but once they reached their home, for some reason she can't comprehend, they started writing her hateful letters.

Minu knew that the friend's story was similar to that of some old fashioned households in India with arranged marriages. Daughters- in-law are not very much liked by in-laws. Her friend further added, that she and her husband have opposite personalities. She is always perky and talkative and her husband serious and sensitive. With time they have better understanding of each other, as they have been married for a long time. They have found love. May be opposite do attract.

In olden times in Indian culture, in laws played a major role in newlyweds couples life. Especially boy's side it always was about a power game. The In laws always interfere to the extent of causing misunderstanding's between the young couple in-law's usually played negative role than positive one in-laws will make false stories to degrade the bride and her side of the family. Those times agenda was to always cause problems and keep fire of misunderstanding and storytelling going. Minu had witnessed few of those experiences, and came to conclusion that family's, who play a negative role, are arrogant, selfish, jealous and not good-hearted people. As they interferes to destroy relationships rather than building strong and loving one. This was mostly prevalent in joint families.

Not all in-laws interfere, now as the times are changing less and less interference is tolerated. More nuclear family's exist. Minu believes in treating all relationships with respect, kindness and love.

Relationships can be challenging, all relationship have some road bumps. If foundation is strong, relationships work out. Minu says sometimes a Sense of self gets complicated, and one has to work harder on keeping one owns individuality. once one feels comfortable in a relationship, one has tendency to take everything for granted. To have open communication is the key to survival of loving and caring relationships All relationships are two way street .She further says, for healthy, happy relationships one must adapt to selective hearing and not sweat on small things. One must avoid micro management ,and have mutual love, and respect for each other.

Chapter 18

Deep in Our Hearts

On August 28, 2011, one phone call changed the life of Minu's younger sister forever. The caller informed her sister that she had lost her oldest son in a car accident on Baton Island close to Singapore, where he had gone for a weekend getaway with his friends. He was a passenger in the car and did not survive.

At the time of this writing, almost eight years have passed, and it is still very painful for Minu to think about what happened on that terrible day. It seems to her that it was only yesterday, and sometimes she catches herself wondering whether it really did happen. Her mind wants to believe that he is still in Singapore studying. When she sees her sister or her brother-in-law and younger nephew, their faces still show the pain they are living with. Minu became a pillar of strength for her heartbroken sister and still talks to her every day.

He was her very first nephew and was born in her hands. Back in India, her sister had been used to maids and nannies, so Minu took on a mother-like role with her newborn nephew, helping her sister care for and nurture him. She fondly remembers giving him many baths, with a massage before each bath, forming a bond that no one can ever break.

Her own two daughters loved to play with her cousin. They too are left with great memories.

Her nephew loved life. He was born with a charismatic personality and a very wise head on his shoulders. At the young age of 21 he had more wisdom than many elderly people. He enjoyed life to the fullest and was adventurous and willing to undertake new and daring tasks.

He also had a very caring heart. His love towards his grandma knew no bounds. He cared about and strove to understand every little one of her likes and dislikes. She was diabetic and he monitored her diet. "Nani" he called her.

He was a guide for his younger brother and for his mom and dad. He is still a guiding light for the entire family.

His leaving has deeply affected each family member, and all miss him greatly. Nearly eight years later, Minu says, with great feeling, "He is still vivid in our memories and will forever be in our hearts. We miss him in our happiness and our sadness. He is part of all of us."

Chapter 19

Regrets, She's Had a Few

Acceptance of her fate has been an elusive target for Minu. Sometimes it is there, sometimes not. Every day we make mistakes, she says, and most of the time we just ignore these failings and move forward. But every so often, there is one that makes us pause and take notice. No one is perfect.

As Minu began to age, her regrets became more intense. They did not fade, as memories do. She sometimes questions whether our lives are predestined, and we are merely walking the path. If she has that thought process, then she says the word *regret* does not exist. It's all life's journey and different experiences.

But when she believes that we make our destiny, then she has regrets, starting with getting married at such a young age.

Regrets for not knowing who she is and what she was born to do. Regrets for never having free thinking. Regrets for not being a high-level professional. She never liked being a physician assistant, as she believed she has a higher level of intelligence and could be a physician. The "assistant" word never sat well with her.

Regrets for moving to a small town. After 36 years, she still wonders how and why her husband picked this place.

Regrets for not knowing how to live her life to the fullest. When she was younger, she did not know how that could be done or what it even meant. Now she is trying to understand and live life in the present.

Regrets for not having individuality.

Regrets for not able to adjust in a small town and the resulting frustrations.

All these regrets are offset by seeing her daughters follow their passion. Her daughters are living her dream. She wants her daughters to live life to the fullest. She does not regret giving her dreams up to nurture her daughters. She would not trade a second spent with her children, as they literally gave meaning to her life. They were, in fact, her lifeline.

Everyone has choices at every step, she says. Each choice we make has ramifications. Her choice was to raise her daughters in a loving home. Afterward there is the empty-nest syndrome to face. She thinks a lot of women her age go through similar situations. That is our generation, she declares, if we are not professionals and follow our husband's life. It is a generation gap.

She believes that as we age, we have a propensity to look back at our lives more than usual, especially if we have nothing of our own to fall back on to keep us happy.

Yet she also reaffirms that believers in destiny have no regrets.

Chapter 20

Acceptance

Finally, after mentally struggling for what has seemed an eternity, Minu has started to accept life the way it is. Yet, in her heart of hearts, she still has the burning desire to be someone and to be known for her abilities and intelligence. Every time she hears about New York or sees something about New York on television, her heart wants to be there.

Her daughters are always on her mind. She remembers loving to watch her younger daughter's television shows when she was in Los Angeles with her. She got hooked on the television drama *Gossip Girl* and was amazed at herself that she stayed up until 4 AM watching episode after episode of the series. Part of the reason was that the entire show was filmed in New York City. As she watched, she sometimes dreamed about what would have happened if she and her husband had never left New York and had built a life on the

Upper East Side. Those thoughts always warmed her heart and made her smile.

She becomes happy whenever her younger daughter takes a few days off her very successful entertainment attorney job in Los Angeles to visit her big sister in New York. At such times, Minu feels that her children are actually living her dream life.

It seems to her at times that she is a lost soul from New York City. How else can she explain her obsession? She even got a New York City physician assistant license. It makes her feel closer to the city, knowing that at least officially, she would be allowed to pursue her career and be productive there.

With her older daughter living in New York City, she gets to go there frequently. When she is there, she wants to build a life there, but she tries hard to accept that for now, life is in California, as her husband has his practice there. She has watched him work so hard, as he is very diligent and a man of integrity. He has earned a name and the respect of his peers. She can't ask him to leave all that, especially as they are getting older. But she always tells her children to live wherever they will be happy.

She is just trying to be realistic about life. She is trying to accept that she will always live in her husband's shadow. While her husband is a physician, she became a physician assistant.

Life after 50 makes Minu think she can no longer dwell on being a dreamer and has to be grateful for all she has. One does not achieve anything by whining. If you want something badly enough, you have to make it happen with diligence and hard work. That is what she taught her daughters. Now she knows it is time for her to listen to her own advice.

So, she has started to take her mother's advice—to live her life being grateful for what she has and acknowledging destiny.

Now her heart waits for her daughters to get married to guys who will worship the ground they walk on. It is only right, as her daughters are themselves truly angels within whose hearts resides warm love and a passion for the well-being of others.

Minu's greatest accomplishment in life, she believes, was raising such pleasing, professional, hard-working daughters.

So, embrace the changes that occur, she thinks. And accept them as positive forces in life that keep you evolving. Enjoy the journey and appreciate that at every step of the way, you can be in a state of constant positive progress. You are always developing into the person you are meant to be.

Today Minu believes that there is much in her life to be thankful for, including a good deal of family bliss. She is happiest when surrounded by her daughters. Life changes as kids grow up and settle far away, with their own dreams and lives to live. Though her older daughter is in New York City and the younger one in Hollywood, she stays connected with them and loves to travel with them.

She has always encouraged her daughters to travel and believes there are several advantages to traveling, as it helps us improve ourselves. Sometimes things don't go according to plan while traveling, especially in this era, so it teaches one to be flexible. It also increases confidence and provides a sense of success. We grow as people, learn new languages, and improve our social skills. Meeting new people is one of travel's great upsides. Exploring new places, we get a better understanding of the people living there, including their culture, customs, history, and background. One can read all the books, but the best way to know about any culture is to go spend time in the country with the people living there.

She also believes traveling can improve overall health and enhance creativity. Therefore, she urges you, the reader, to take time out from your daily tasks, office responsibilities, hectic schedule, and everyday pressures at least once in a year. Plan a tour, with an open schedule, to a new city, and let life present you with numerous opportunities to widen your horizons. No matter how young or old you are, there is always a time when the child in you wants to have some fun. When you travel, you need not care at all what you do, and you can just break free from the norm.

Minu plans an international trip once a year with her precious daughters and husband. She believes a family that travels together stays together. Travel with family helps you build stronger bonds and make memories. You can also save those memories by creating photo albums or sharing photos. Every year she and her family choose one destination and spend a week. Every country she visited with her family has left an everlasting impression. Together, they have been to Austria, Italy, France, Hungary, Paraguay, Australia, and Scotland. In Africa they took a safari for a breathtaking vacation, watching animals in their natural habitat. Priceless.

She and her family also play tennis, and they love to watch the sport. Their family tradition for over ten years has been to go watch the U.S. Open at Flushing Meadows in New York.

Time spent with her daughters and husband taking vacations and watching sports is priceless. She believes in traveling internationally while still young. Once one is older and can't fly for long hours, then is the time to explore one's own country.

She read somewhere that life doesn't have to be as hard as it may sometimes seem. There's an art to learning to let things go and leaving the worries of the past behind with yesterday. In life we are all carrying a heavy load, yet what differentiates us is how we choose to carry it. Those who go through life with a seemingly unaffected attitude are the people who understand the angles of life and the difference between what can be changed and what cannot. In understanding that difference, they are able to move on and enjoy life as it is presented. Life is too short to be fretting over things that cannot be changed and not to be making the best out of situations.

Learn to adjust your expectations and change your outlook so you don't waste moments that could have been great ones.

Today Minu says, and believes:

Accept your fate, change your journey.

Whatever happens, happens. It's a simple saying, but it's a simple concept. The things that happen in life cannot always be explained or changed, but you can change the path you take to them. Fate has a way of showing us that we aren't always in control over what happens to us, but it also tells us that we can make our own path, even if we can't see where it will lead. If you want to change what's happening to you, change your path.

Accept where you are now, change where you are going.

You may not like where you are now, but that doesn't mean you don't have the power to change where you're going. Only the weak let their current situation determine their future one. The strong and the passionate take charge of their future and don't let their surroundings stop them from getting somewhere else.

Accept the choices you've made, change your next ones.

Holding on to regrets is like bringing a jar full of bees into your house. There's no need for them and they will only end up stinging you.

To My Daughters

E very Mother's Day and on her daughters' birthdays,
Minu writes a letter to them and finds herself talking
like her Mom. Here is a recent letter she wrote to them:

My wonderful daughters,

I write this letter with gratitude.

*I am so proud of you, my two beautiful
daughters. You are my world and an inspiration
to today's young women. You have proved that
with hard work, focus, and perseverance people
can attain their dreams. Today I am so proud
that you have become a successful entertainment
lawyer and an interventional cardiologist.*

You each have such a demanding, successful, and stressful career. Yet you conduct your lives with balance.

Mothers will always be mothers, so I have few words of advice for you as life unfolds.

Always have time for yourself, love your own company. Unplug technology regularly and get away.

Cultivate your hobbies, play your guitars. Find time to play tennis and do yoga. Meditate.

Have time for gym on a regular basis.

It's very important to have the ability to handle adverse situations and the strength to do so. Embrace change. Remember what the great physicist Albert Einstein is reputed to have said: "Life is like riding a bicycle; to keep your balance, you have to keep moving."

Live in the present. Never live in fear.

Do your best and leave the rest.

Life is day and night, it does not always go as planned, so always have courage and flexibility to roll with the punches. Be open minded.

Never let work affect how you relate to your family.

Trust your inner voice, your intuition. Be confident in yourselves.

No one knows you completely, no one knows how it feels to be you. So, don't set yourself up for disappointment. Your happiness is up to you.

You don't have to prove anything to anyone. Just be true to yourself.

Learn to say "no" to others, as we often pass our lives saying "yes, yes, yes" to others. That was your mom at a younger age, always wanting to fit in and please people. I learned later on the hard way.

Don't do what you have to force yourself into. Don't allow yourself to be drawn into battles you don't want to fight. Pick the battles you are sure to win. It is easier to get into things than get out.

When in difficult situations, tell yourself, "This shall pass. Nothing lasts forever."

In a wise book it has been said that you become what you think the most. So, think the thoughts that make you happy and feel good. Positive thinkers have the power to be creative. A positive attitude means progress. Be positive but not pollyannaish (foolishly optimistic). Negative thinkers are often gloomy and pessimistic.

Don't judge yourself; instead, promote yourself.

Always be careful what you wish for is an old and astute saying.

Take frequent vacations and enjoy nature and the outdoors. The world is sooo very beautiful. Traveling makes us grow as a person. Live life to the fullest. Celebrate life, make it thrilling.

Always take care of your health. Be proactive.

Always be grateful for what you have, focus on what you have. Stay centered. Wake up in the morning with the thought that all is well all and all will be well; I am going to have joyous day. Let love, light, and life surround you at all times.

On the lighter side, don't forget to enjoy good wine with each other, my daughters, you are each other's strength and soul mate. My existence is you both.

Someday, when you become mothers, just remember to love your children unconditionally, give them wings to fly, teach them discipline and self-love. Put them first. At the same time, don't live your life through them. That's what my mom taught me, but I paid too little attention to her advice. There are so many things I wish I had learned early on in life. Motherhood is the greatest and the hardest thing.

My daughters, my everything. My world, my sunshine.

My heart, my dreams.

My reflection, my inspiration. My joy, my life.

My greatest gift.

My daughters, the meaning of my life.

Today, Minu is living her life filled with gratitude and acceptance. Yet, she declares that acceptance is not acquiescence. She still retains the passion of her youth and strives to understand her destiny. And, as ever, she strives to be and do her very best on her life's journey. This includes her supporting various nonprofit organizations. She also works to be an advocate and speaker for preventive medicine, which has led her to develop a health- focused blog on her website, www.healthandempower.com. She is passionate about her blog, hoping readers will empower themselves with awareness of how disease can be prevented by healthy living.

She considers her husband to be her soul mate. Through all the differences, their love and caring for each other grew stronger, and they became each other's strength. In a true sense, her relationship with her husband is, for her, till death do us part.

sss

Printed in the United States
By Bookmasters